ADOPTED FOR A PURPOSE

ADOPTED FOR A PURPOSE

Bible Stories of Joseph, Moses, Samuel, and Esther

Pauline Youd

Abingdon Press

Nashville

ADOPTED FOR A PURPOSE

BIBLE STORIES OF JOSEPH, MOSES, SAMUEL, AND ESTHER

Copyright © 1986 by Abingdon Press

This book is printed on acid-free paper.

Library of Congress Cataloging-in-Publication Data

YOUD, PAULINE, 1932-
    Adopted for a purpose.

    Summary: Presents the Bible stories of Joseph, Moses,
Samuel, and Esther, all of whom were taken from their
natural parents and raised by someone else.
    1. Joseph (son of Jacob)—Juvenile literature.
    2. Moses (biblical leader)—Juvenile literature.
    3. Samuel (biblical judge)—Juvenile literature.
    4. Esther, Queen of Persia—Juvenile literature.
    5. Bible. O.T.—Biography—Juvenile literature.
    6. Bible stories, English—O.T. [1. Joseph (son of
    Jacob) 2. Moses (biblical leader) 3. Samuel (biblical
    judge) 4. Esther, Queen of Persia. 5. Bible stories—
    O.T.] I. Title.
BS551.2.Y63   1986   221.9'22   86-3598

ISBN 0-687-00770-4

(alk. paper)

Scripture quotations marked (NIV) are from the Holy Bible, New
International Version. Copyright © 1973, 1978, 1984, International
Bible Society. Used by permission of Zondervan Bible Publishers.

Those noted Amplified are from the Amplified Old Testament, Part
One. Copyright © 1964 by Zondervan Publishing House.

MANUFACTURED BY THE PARTHENON PRESS AT
NASHVILLE, TENNESSEE, UNITED STATES OF AMERICA

To

Tracy

Our adopted daughter

My special thanks to Cathy Grindheim
for her invaluable secretarial assistance in
typing and retyping this manuscript.

Pauline Youd
July 1985

CONTENTS

EACH ONE UNIQUE

Although my father and my mother have forsaken me, yet the Lord will take me up *and* adopt me as His child" (Psalm 27:10 Amplified).

"I was cast upon You from my very birth; from my mother's womb You are my God" (Psalm 22:10 Amplified).

"Why couldn't my parents keep me?" "What were the circumstances of my birth?" "What are my real 'roots'?"

This book may not answer all your personal questions about adoption for that is not its real purpose. It does show, however, how God uses what we may regard as undesirable circumstances for his greater purposes.

Each of the four Bible characters, Joseph, Moses, Samuel, and Esther, were taken by God from their natural parents and raised by someone else. Joseph was actually thrust out upon God alone. Moses was raised by Pharaoh's daughter. Samuel was trained by Eli, the priest. Esther lived with her older cousin.

Each character left his or her natural family at a different time in life. Joseph was seventeen years old. Moses was an infant. Samuel was a young child, probably around five years old. The Bible does not say how old Esther was but she was probably a preteen.

Each character left his or her natural family under different circumstances. Joseph was sold as a slave by his jealous brothers. Moses' mother gave him to the Egyptian Pharaoh's daughter in order to save his life. Samuel's mother gave her son back to God because she had promised that she would if God gave her a son. Esther lived with her cousin, Mordecai, because her parents had died.

What happened to each of these people? Joseph entered a strange land where his own belief in the one true God was not taught. He had no other believers with whom to have fellowship, but he believed God was real so he began to live out his faith. From his infancy Moses lived in Pharaoh's courts and had the best Egyptian education available. He didn't know until he was an adult that he was a Hebrew or that he had been adopted. Samuel was reared in the temple. He knew his family but he only saw them once a year. Eli, the priest, became his guardian and guided him to his special purpose which was to serve God. Esther's family had been taken captive by the

Babylonians when they conquered Jerusalem. Esther was born while they were refugees. When her parents died leaving Esther an orphan, she was adopted by her older cousin, Mordecai. Mordecai shrewdly helped Esther become queen of Persia.

With that brief introduction, let's begin these fascinating stories. Perhaps you'll find some of your circumstances written here. Perhaps you'll find some comfort, some courage, and some challenges along the way. It is hoped that you will trust God more with your life when you have seen how God worked in the lives of Joseph, who was never bitter with his circumstances; Moses, whose secular training was not wasted; Samuel, who had pure devotion to God; and Esther, who was guided by God's coincidences.

ADOPTED FOR A PURPOSE

1.

NEVER BITTER

I

Joseph was the eleventh son of Jacob. What was God's plan for this child? Joseph was the first son born to Rachel, Jacob's favorite wife. How would God train him to lead the nation of Israel? How would Joseph respond to the lessons God would teach him?

Joseph's father, Jacob, had two wives. He had worked for seven years to win Rachel as his bride but when his new wife removed her veil, Jacob discovered he had married Leah, Rachel's older sister. Leah and Rachel's father said it was not right for the younger daughter to marry before the older one, so he gave Leah to Jacob. However he said if Jacob really wanted

Rachel too, he could work for seven more years. Jacob agreed and ended up with two wives.

To make matters worse Leah began to have children, and Rachel did not. "See, I have given Jacob a son," she proudly announced to Rachel. In fact Leah bore four sons: Reuben, Levi, Simeon, and Judah. With each successive birth Rachel became more anxious and envious. Leah, of course, didn't make things easier. "I don't believe you'll ever have children," she taunted.

Finally, Rachel could stand it no longer so she devised what she thought was an acceptable plan.

She thought, perhaps Bilhah, my maid, could have children and I could take them as my own. So Rachel sent Bilhah, her maid, to Jacob. Bilhah did conceive and had a son who she named Dan. Then she had another son, Naphtali. But when Leah saw what Rachel had done, she too sent her maid, Zilpah, to Jacob. Zilpah had a son and named him Gad. In time she too had a second son, Asher. Then Leah became pregnant again. Over the next few years she had two more sons, Issachar and Zebulun, and one daughter, Dinah. Jacob now had ten sons and one daughter!

Finally, Rachel had children of her own: Joseph and Benjamin. This completed Jacob's family and this was the family in which Joseph was reared. Joseph had ten older brothers, one older sister, and one younger brother, but he was still the firstborn son of his father's favorite wife. Therefore Jacob loved Joseph more than any of his other sons. In fact, Jacob gave Joseph a special long coat with sleeves to wear instead of a short no-sleeved tunic like the ones his brothers wore.

As Joseph grew, God began to give him dreams about his future. Joseph and his family may not have known that these were prophetical dreams but Joseph took delight in telling them to his brothers and father as they sat around the evening fire.

In one dream all the brothers were binding sheaves of grain in the field.

"My sheaf stood upright and all the others bowed to it," declared Joseph.

The brothers immediately sensed that Joseph was saying one day they would bow to him and their resentment toward this favorite son grew.

In another dream Joseph said the sun, moon, and stars bowed to him. When Jacob heard this he scolded Joseph for being disrespectful, for Joseph was saying that his father and mother as well as his brothers would bow down to him.

One day Jacob sent Joseph on an errand to check on his brothers who were pasturing their flocks some distance from home. When the brothers looked up and saw Joseph dressed in his long coat coming toward them, they became angry.

"Here comes the dreamer," one of them called scornfully. Together they decided to kill Joseph and tell their father that some ferocious beast had eaten him.

When Joseph approached in his usual casual manner, the brothers closed in on him, jumped on him, and threw him to the ground.

"Get him," shouted one.

"Hold him," yelled another.

"Take off that coat!"

"Kill him."

But Reuben tried to persuade them not to kill Joseph. Since he was the oldest, he would be the one responsible to his father for Joseph. So the brothers stripped Joseph of his long coat and threw him into an empty pit. Then as he questioned and cried and pleaded with his brothers, they simply sat down to eat their lunch.

While they sat there they saw a caravan in the distance. They recognized the tradesmen as Ishmaelites carrying spices along the route from Gilead to Egypt. Then Judah had an idea.

"What do we gain if we kill him?" he said pointing to Joseph. "Let's sell him to the Ishmaelites. Maybe they'd like a young slave. Then," he added, "we won't have killed our own brother."

The brothers quickly agreed. They pulled Joseph up out of the pit and for twenty pieces of silver sold him to the Ishmaelites. Then with Joseph still reaching out to his brothers for help, the caravan proceeded on its way to Egypt, not knowing or caring about the circumstances surrounding the new slave.

The brothers watched until the caravan was out of sight. Then hardly looking at one another, they killed a young goat, dipped Joseph's long coat into the blood and took the coat to their father.

Jacob recognized at once the coat he had given to Joseph.

"A wild animal has devoured my son," he cried out in anguish.

The brothers, of course, knew differently but they said nothing, letting their father believe Joseph had been killed and eaten by some wild animal.

During the following days, no matter how they tried to console their father, he would not be comforted.

You Decide

1. *How do you think the brothers felt when Joseph was given the long coat with sleeves?*

2. *If you were Joseph and knew your brothers resented you, how would you try to make them like you?*

3. *Do you think Joseph enjoyed his position of favorite son?*

4. Do you think people ought to be sold as slaves?

5. Describe what you imagine the life of a slave is like.

II

Meanwhile the Ishmaelites arrived in Egypt and sold Joseph to Potiphar, the captain and chief executioner of the royal guard of Pharaoh.

Joseph, who was only seventeen, cowered in fright. His heart raced wildly but his body was strangely paralyzed.

What will this man do to me? he thought. I want to go home to my father.

His hands clenched into fists and his jaw tightened. He fought to keep back hot tears of frustration and anger.

"My own brothers sold me and they were going to kill me. How could they do this?" he asked over and over.

With many miles separating him from his family, Joseph turned to God whom he had been taught to worship since his youth. But God knew all along what was happening to Joseph and God was with him all the way to Egypt, carefully guiding each step, even his sale to Potiphar.

Potiphar saw that God was with Joseph and that everything he did flourished and succeeded. In fact Joseph pleased Potiphar so much that he put Joseph in charge of his entire household and all that he had. God blessed all that Potiphar had in his house and in his fields because of Joseph.

After a while Potiphar's wife noticed that Joseph was a very attractive man, and she tried to tempt Joseph to make love to her, but he refused.

"My master has trusted me with all that he has and you are his wife," he said. "How then could I do such an evil thing and sin against God?"

Joseph knew that by making love to Potiphar's wife he would not only be sinning against Potiphar but also against God who had cared for him in this strange land.

But day after day she tempted Joseph until one day she grabbed the garment he was wearing. Joseph left his garment in her hand and ran out of the house. Joseph was not a coward or a prude. He was very wise. He was also obedient to God.

Potiphar's wife, however, was furious. She called her servants.

"See what the Hebrew servant has done," she shrieked. "He came in to make love to me but I screamed and I cried and he ran away. See, he even left his clothes here in my hand."

She laid the garment aside until her husband got home and then she repeated the lie to him.

"This Hebrew servant whom you brought

here came in to insult me by trying to make love to me. I screamed for help as loud as I could and he finally ran out leaving his clothes here."

When Potiphar heard that and saw the evidence in his wife's hand, he was enraged and he had Joseph thrown into prison.

You Decide

1. *When Potiphar had Joseph thrown into prison, how do you think Joseph felt?*
2. *If this was a test of Joseph's obedience, did he pass the test?*
3. *What was his reward?*
4. *How would Joseph know that God was still around and was guiding his life?*

III

God was with Joseph even in prison and whatever he did went well. The jail warden soon trusted Joseph so much that he put all the prisoners in Joseph's charge and paid no more attention to them.

Sometime later Pharaoh's chief butler and chief baker offended him. He had them both put in prison and the captain of the guard put them in Joseph's care.

One night the chief butler and the chief baker had dreams that disturbed them. In the morning when Joseph came in, he saw both of them depressed and sad.

"Why do you look so dejected and sad this morning?" he asked them.

"We have dreamed dreams," they answered, "and there is no one to interpret them."

They thought that only the wise men and magicians of the land could interpret dreams, and there were no wise men or magicians in prison.

"Don't interpretations belong to God?" asked Joseph. "Tell me your dreams."

They must have recognized that God was with Joseph because they didn't hesitate to tell him what they had dreamed.

"I saw a vine with three branches," began the chief butler, "and the vine budded, then blossomed, and then produced grapes. I squeezed the grapes into Pharaoh's cup and gave the cup to Pharaoh."

"This is the interpretation," said Joseph. "The three branches are three days. In three days Pharaoh will restore you to your position of chief butler and once again you will put Pharaoh's cup into his hand."

Joseph quickly added, "But think of me after you have regained your position. Be kind to me by mentioning me to Pharaoh so that I may be released from this prison. For first I was carried away from my Hebrew land unlawfully, and now here I have done nothing for which they should put me in prison."

When the chief baker saw that the interpretation of the chief butler's dream was good, he also told Joseph his dream.

"I had three cake baskets on my head," he said. "In the top basket were all kinds of baked foods for Pharaoh. But birds of prey were eating out of the basket on my head."

Joseph looked steadily at the chief baker.

"I am sad to tell you this," he said, "but I will be honest before God. The three baskets are three days. In three days Pharaoh will call for you but he will have you beheaded and hung on a tree." Joseph hesitated. "You won't even be buried, but the birds will eat your flesh."

Sure enough, on the third day, Pharaoh's birthday, he gave a feast for all his servants, and he called for the chief butler and the chief baker. He did restore the chief butler to his job as Joseph had said, but he hanged the chief baker.

Even after all that, the chief butler forgot all about Joseph. God was still teaching Joseph to trust in him, not in what men could do for him.

You Decide

1. How did God speak to the chief butler, the chief baker, and Pharaoh?
2. Who interpreted the dreams?

IV

After two years the chief butler finally remembered his promise to Joseph.

One night Pharaoh was awakened from his sleep by a bad dream. For a while he lay there trying to imagine what it meant. Finally he fell asleep again but was awakened by another bad dream. Pharaoh was so upset that he called for all the magicians and wise men in Egypt. When they came, he told them his dreams but no one could interpret them. Then the chief butler came forward.

"I remember my past sins," he said. "When you were angry with me and had the chief baker and me put in prison, we both dreamed dreams one night. There was a young Hebrew man in the prison who interpreted our dreams and they came to pass exactly as he said. I was restored to my office as chief butler and the chief baker was hanged."

Immediately Pharaoh sent for Joseph. Joseph had waited and prayed for this moment for a long time. But now he took time to shave his Hebrew beard, change his clothes, and make himself presentable before going to Pharaoh.

"I have heard that you can interpret dreams," said Pharaoh when Joseph approached his throne. "I have dreamed a dream but no one can interpret it for me."

"It is not in me, O Pharaoh, to interpret dreams," answered Joseph. "God will give you an answer so you can have peace."

Pharaoh told Joseph his dream.

"I stood on the bank of the Nile River," he said, "and seven sleek, fat cows came out and began grazing. Then seven thin, ugly cows like I've never seen in all Egypt came out and ate the fat cows, but they didn't get any fatter as a result."

He paused for a moment and then continued.

"I woke up, but as I slept again I had another dream. I saw seven full, plump ears of grain growing on one stalk. Then seven other ears which were thin and ruined by the wind sprouted after them and they devoured the seven full, plump ears."

Pharaoh leaned back on his throne and said, "These were my dreams and no one can tell me what they mean."

"The two dreams mean the same thing," began Joseph. "God is showing you what is going to happen. The seven fat cows and the seven full ears of grain are seven years. The seven thin cows and the seven ruined ears of grain are also seven years but ones of hunger or famine. God is showing you that soon there will be seven years of abundant crops. These will be followed by seven years of a famine so severe that the seven good years will be forgotten. God sent the dream twice so you'd know it is from him and that it will happen soon."

The wise men began nodding and talking excitedly with one another. Pharaoh raised his hand for silence for Joseph had more to say.

"The Pharaoh should choose a man to be in charge and to appoint officers over the land," Joseph advised. "He should gather one-fifth of all the grain produced in each of the seven good years. This should be stored so it can be used during the seven years of hunger and famine."

"Can we find any man like this man?" Pharaoh asked his wise men. "The Spirit of God is in him."

Then turning to Joseph he said, "Since your God has shown you all this, there is no one as understanding and wise as you are. You will be the man in charge, and all my people will do whatever you tell them to do. Only in matters of the throne will I be greater than you."

Then standing he said, "I now set you over the whole land of Egypt."

Pharaoh gave Joseph his signet ring to sign and seal his orders and fine robes to wear and a gold chain to hang around his neck. He made him ride in the second chariot, the one right after his own, and had officials cry before him, "Bow the knee!" Furthermore he gave Asenath, the daughter of the priest of On, to him to be his wife.

Joseph, who was now thirty years old, was in charge of all Egypt.

The seven good years came and there were abundant crops. Joseph gathered up all the surplus grain from the fields and stored it in the cities. When the seven good and abundant years ended, the seven years of famine came just as Joseph had said. The famine was severe in all the surrounding countries, but in Egypt there was the grain that had been stored up by Joseph. The people of Egypt began to buy grain from Joseph and as the word spread, people from the surrounding nations also came to buy grain.

You Decide

1. *Who was responsible for Joseph's getting out of prison?*
2. *Who recognized that God was with Joseph?*

V

Up in Canaan, Jacob learned that there was grain to be had in Egypt. He decided to send his sons to buy grain for the family because the famine extended even to Canaan. He did not send Benjamin, Joseph's full brother, because he didn't want any harm to come to him.

The brothers took wagons and sacks for grain and made the long, dusty trip to Egypt using the same route the Ishmaelites had used years before when they carried Joseph away from his home. When the brothers arrived they went to

Joseph to buy the grain. Not knowing who he was, they bowed down before him making their request.

Joseph recognized his brothers immediately and his heart leaped inside him. My brothers, he thought. They have come for grain.

One by one he studied them and called their names in his mind. *Benjamin. Where is Benjamin? He is not with them.*

His thoughts raced back to when his brothers out of jealousy had thrown him into the pit. Had they gotten rid of Benjamin too? He must find out.

"Where do you come from?" he asked them through his interpreter. His voice was rough and harsh.

"From Canaan to buy grain," they answered, not daring to rise from their humble position.

Joseph remembered the dreams he had dreamed about them.

"No," he said, "you are spies. You have come to see how desolate our land is."

The brothers must really have been stunned at this.

"Oh no, my Lord," they answered. "We are all the sons of one man. We are honest men and have only come to buy grain."

But Joseph, seeking more information, persisted.

"No, you are spies and have come to see the nakedness of our land."

The brothers again protested.

29

"Your servants are twelve brothers, the sons of one man in Canaan. The youngest is with our father and one is no more."

That indeed was an interesting statement. When they didn't really know what had happened to their brother after they had sold him they said, "He is no more."

Joseph still pretended not to believe them.

"I'll let you prove your story," he said. "One of you can go and get the brother at home while the rest stay in prison."

With that he put them all in prison for three days. There in the same prison where Joseph had spent several years of his life, the brothers had plenty of time to think. Would they be killed and never see their home and families again? What could they do to make this governor of Egypt believe them?

On the third day they were once again brought before Joseph.

"Do this and live," he said. "I fear God. If you are honest men, let one man remain here in prison for surety and the rest of you carry grain to the hungry ones in your households. But bring your youngest brother back here so your words can be verified and you can live."

The brothers began to talk to one another, not knowing that Joseph could understand them. "We are truly guilty about our brother. We saw his anguish and heard his pleading to let him go, but we would not listen. Now this difficulty has come on us."

"Didn't I tell you not to sin against the boy?" said Reuben. "But you wouldn't listen. Now his blood is required of us."

When Joseph heard this, he turned and went away and wept. When he returned he took Simeon, the next oldest after Reuben, and had him bound before their eyes.

Then Joseph secretly told his servant to load the men's sacks with grain and also to put the money they paid for it back into their sacks.

With heavy hearts the brothers loaded their donkeys and began their journey home. When they stopped for the night, one of the brothers opened his sack to get grain for his donkey, and he caught sight of the money.

"My money has been returned," he shouted. "It is here in my sack."

The other brothers ran to him and looked in disbelief. Then each opened his sack and found that his money also had been returned.

"What is this that God is doing to us?" they asked trembling.

They continued their journey home. Finally, after many days they arrived and told their father everything that had happened. Jacob, too, was afraid, especially when they told him they were to prove their honesty by taking Benjamin back to Egypt with them.

"You have bereaved me!" wailed Jacob. "Joseph is gone and Simeon is gone and now you want to take Benjamin from me."

"I will personally keep Benjamin with me," Reuben offered, "and I will return him to you. You can even kill my two sons if I do not bring Benjamin back to you."

Jacob answered, "He shall not go for he is the only one left of his mother's children. If anything should happen to him I would grieve until I die."

You Decide

1. *Why did Joseph accuse his brothers of being spies?*

2. *Why did Joseph have the brothers' money put back in their sacks?*

3. *Why do you think it helped the brothers to know that this governor of Egypt feared God?*

VI

The famine persisted in Canaan as well as in Egypt and the surrounding countries and soon Jacob and his family were once again nearly out of food. So Jacob said to his sons, "Go to Egypt again and buy some grain for us."

"It's of no use to go unless we take Benjamin with us," argued Judah. "The man sternly warned us that he would not even take the time to hear us if we didn't bring Benjamin."

"Why did you tell the man you had another brother?" cried Jacob.

"He asked us straightforward questions," said Judah. "He asked, 'Is your father still alive?' and 'Have you another brother?' We simply answered his questions. How were we to know he would ask us to bring him down there?"

Jacob sat silently, his head bowed in his hands.

"Send Benjamin with me so we and our families can live and not die," pleaded Judah. "I will be responsible for him. If I do not bring him back to you, then I will bear the blame forever. Besides," he added, "if we hadn't waited so long we could have been there and back by now."

Jacob relented and said they could take Benjamin.

"Take some of our best products with you," he said sadly. "Take some balm, some honey, some spices, and some nuts. Take double the price needed for the grain and also take the money that was returned in your sacks. Perhaps it was an oversight. May God give you mercy and favor before the man so he may release Simeon and also Benjamin to you."

He turned away.

"If I am bereaved, I am bereaved."

The next morning the brothers loaded the gifts on the donkeys, took the extra money and Benjamin, and journeyed to Egypt again.

When they arrived and Joseph saw Benjamin with his brothers, he told his steward to prepare a noon meal for them to eat with him. This frightened the brothers for this was indeed different treatment from anyone else who was there buying grain. They thought Joseph's steward had somehow found out about the money in their sacks.

Seeing the steward at the door, they approached him and said, "Sir, the first time we came here it really was to buy grain. On the way home we found each man's money in his sack along with the grain. We have brought it back with us and we've brought other money to buy more grain. We don't know how the money got in our sacks."

"Don't worry," the steward reassured them. "Your God has given you treasure in your sacks. I received your money."

Then he brought Simeon out to them. The Bible doesn't say how long he had been in prison or how he had been treated but you can be sure that Joseph was kept informed about his health and care.

At noon the brothers were brought before Joseph and again they bowed down to him and presented their gifts.

"Is your old father still well?" Joseph asked. "You spoke of him the last time you were here. Is he still alive?"

"Yes, he is alive and in good health," they answered.

Then Joseph turned to Benjamin and said, "And is this your youngest brother of whom you spoke?"

He touched Benjamin and said, "God be gracious to you, my son."

With that Joseph hurriedly left the room and wept privately. He had finally seen his brother again.

A few minutes later he returned and said, "Let dinner be served."

There were three tables in the dining room. One was set for Joseph to be served alone. From there he sent food to the other tables. The brothers were seated at another table arranged in order from the oldest to the youngest, and they wondered how this information could be known. The Egyptians occupied the remaining table, not eating with the Hebrews because their custom didn't allow it.

As the dinner progressed, Joseph sent food to his brothers, but he sent five times as much to Benjamin as he did to anyone else.

After dinner Joseph commanded his steward to load the brothers' sacks with grain and again include their money.

"One other thing," he added. "Put my silver cup in Benjamin's sack."

You Decide

1. *When Jacob finally sent Benjamin with his brothers to Egypt, do you think he ever expected to see him again?*

2. *While Simeon was in prison, do you think he suspected anything out of the ordinary?*

3. *What puzzling things happened to the brothers?*

4. *How would you feel if these things had happened to you?*

VII

Early the next morning the brothers set out for home. They had not gone far when Joseph called his steward again and said, "Go after them and say, 'Why have you given evil for good? One of you has stolen my master's silver cup.' "

When the steward overtook the brothers and told them the things Joseph had commanded him to say, the brothers were shocked.

"We would not do such a thing," they cried. "You saw how we returned the money the first time. Why then would we now take silver or gold from your master?"

Finally, because they were so positive none of them had stolen the cup, one offered, "We'll open our sacks and you can search them. The one in whose grain you find the cup should be killed and the others of us will be your slaves."

"We'll do as you say," agreed the steward, "but the one in whose grain the cup is found will be my slave. The others can go free."

So they opened the sacks and the steward searched them from the eldest to the youngest.

In Benjamin's sack he found the silver cup. In agony the brothers tore their clothes as a sign of grief. Then very slowly loading their donkeys, they again returned to Joseph's house. Coming before him, they fell brokenly at his feet.

"What is this you have done?" Joseph asked coolly. "Didn't you know I could find you out?"

"What can we possibly say in our defense?" Judah responded woefully. "God has found out and revealed our sin. We will surely all become your slaves."

"No," Joseph answered, "only the one in whose sack the cup was found will be my slave. The rest of you may return home to your father."

Then Judah came close to Joseph and imploringly asked if he could talk to him privately.

"Please don't be angry, but you are as Pharaoh and I will talk as if I were talking directly to him," he said. "When we came here the first time you asked if we had a father or a brother and we answered you honestly. You also told us that we could not come back and get more grain unless we brought our youngest brother, even though we told you he was the only son left of the wife his father had loved dearly. We told you he could not leave his old father because if he did, his father would die, but you said we could not see your face again unless we brought him. When we returned home, we told our father what you said. When in time he again asked us to go to Egypt to buy food, we reminded him that we could not go without Benjamin. He said, 'Rachel, my wife, bore me two sons. One surely was torn to pieces and I have never seen him since. If you take the other one and an accident befalls him, I will grieve until I die.' Now when we return and he sees the lad is not with us, the one whom he loves dearly, he will surely die and we will be responsible for his death. I, myself, became surety for the lad and told my father that if I didn't bring him back I would bear the blame forever."

Judah fell on his knees before Joseph.

"Please," he begged, "let me remain here now and be your slave so Benjamin can go home with his brothers to his father. For how can I face my father without him?"

As Judah spoke, Joseph could see how much the brothers had changed in their compassion for their father and for their brother, Benjamin. He knew God had spoken to them concerning their sin toward him. He also began to understand that God had sent him to Egypt. And now he couldn't restrain himself any longer.

Joseph made everyone except his brothers leave the room.

"I am Joseph," he said fervently. "Is my father still alive?"

The brothers could not reply because of their shock and dismay at this news.

"Come to me," said Joseph weeping openly. "I am your brother Joseph whom you sold into Egypt. Don't be distressed and angry with yourselves because you sold me here, for it was God who sent me and made me lord of Pharaoh's house and ruler over all Egypt."

The brothers still stared in disbelief.

"So far there have been two years of famine," Joseph continued, "but there will be five more. God wants to save your lives. He wants to continue a remnant from Abraham upon the earth, so he sent me here before you to preserve your descendants."

One by one the brothers began to nod in recognition.

"Hurry! Go tell my father that I am in charge of all Egypt," urged Joseph. "Come down here and you shall live with all your families in Goshen. It is near me. I can provide for all of you during the years of famine that are still coming."

Then he approached Benjamin and said, "See how Benjamin and I look alike? Hear me. I am talking in your own language and not through an interpreter."

Then his brothers realized that it was really Joseph. They also knew that he had understood all of their conversations from the first time they had met, even when they talked about what they had done to him and how God must be punishing them.

Joseph and Benjamin embraced each other and wept. Then Joseph kissed all his brothers and they began talking together.

When Pharaoh was told that Joseph's brothers had come, he invited them all, with their families and their father to come and live in Egypt. He gave orders that wagons and food provisions should be given them for their trip.

It was Joseph who saw that everything was loaded and ready when at last it was time to leave. He gave each brother changes of clothes but he gave five changes of clothes plus three hundred pieces of silver to Benjamin. Knowing what such partiality had cost in his life, Joseph was perhaps providing a further test for the brothers.

"Don't quarrel along the way," he called after them as they left.

You Decide

1. *Why did Joseph have his steward put his silver cup in Benjamin's sack?*
2. *Did the brothers defend themselves before Joseph? Why?/Why not?*
3. *Who did they think was punishing them?*
4. *Why did Joseph continue to show partiality to Benjamin when it had caused such problems in his own life?*
5. *What do you think Joseph was trying to learn from his brothers?*

VIII

The brothers went back to Canaan and their father. Jacob was anxiously awaiting their return but was not prepared for what he heard them say when they saw him.

"Joseph is alive. He is governor over all Egypt. He is second in command under Pharaoh."

The shock was too much and Jacob became faint. He wouldn't believe them until he saw all the wagons and the provisions that followed. Then he believed.

"It is enough," he said. "Joseph, my son, is alive. I must go to see him before I die."

Hurriedly they began the preparations to move their families to Egypt. Seventy people in all, with their flocks and herds and goods, finally began the long journey. At Beersheba, which was on the way, they stopped and offered sacrifices to God. While there God spoke to Jacob in a dream.

"Don't be afraid to go to Egypt," he said, "for I will bring your descendants back again to Canaan. You will die in your old age in Egypt with Joseph at your side."

As they neared their destination, Jacob sent Judah ahead to Joseph so he could direct them to Goshen and meet them there.

Imagine what a meeting that must have been! Joseph, dressed in his rich robes, met them and presented himself to his aged father. Proving that he indeed was Joseph, he and his family wept together for a long time.

The Bible never says that Jacob was angry and bitter against his sons for selling Joseph, but think of all the years he had missed being with his favorite son and watching him mature to manhood. Joseph had forgiven his brothers and had realized how he fit into God's plan for his people, so Jacob must have done so too. Before Joseph went to tell Pharaoh that his family had arrived, he instructed his brothers that when they met Pharaoh they should say they were keepers of livestock in order that they might live in Goshen. Goshen was a special part of Egypt where God knew the Hebrews could remain a separate people. Egyptians did not like shepherds at all so this was a good reason for them to want to be separated.

Joseph picked five of his brothers to present to Pharaoh, and Pharaoh gave them the land of Goshen. He further charged Joseph that if there were men in his family who were skillful with cattle, they should be put in charge of his cattle.

Then Joseph presented his father to Pharaoh. Jacob blessed Pharaoh.

"How old are you?" Pharaoh asked Jacob, affectionately.

"I am one hundred and thirty years old," replied Jacob, "but my forefathers lived much longer than that."

After this, Jacob lived seventeen more years in Egypt. Then he became sick and Joseph was called to his bedside. Joseph came bringing his two sons, Manasseh and Ephraim.

"I didn't think I'd ever see your face again," said Jacob, "but now God has let me see your sons also. These sons who were born to you in Egypt before I came, I'm now adopting as my own sons. They will inherit the same as the sons born to me."

Joseph took them close to his father for Jacob to bless them.

"They shall both be great nations," Jacob said, placing his hands on them, "but the younger shall be greater than the elder."

Leaning back on his bed, Jacob made one request of Joseph. Jacob did not want to be buried in Egypt. He wanted his body returned to Canaan and buried with Abraham and Isaac.

After Jacob died and he was mourned seventy days in Egypt, Joseph requested that Pharaoh allow him to take his father's body back to Canaan to bury him. Pharaoh gave him permission, and Joseph and his family, except for the young children, went to bury Jacob in Canaan. In tribute to Joseph a great many Egyptians also accompanied them.

After Joseph buried his father, they returned to Egypt. Then his brothers began to be afraid again. "Perhaps now Joseph will hate us and pay us back for the evil we did to him," they reasoned.

They sent Joseph this message: "Before our father died, he told us to ask you to forgive us for our sin, so now we do ask. Please forgive us for the evil we did to you."

They dressed in clean clothes and went to see Joseph and fell down before him saying, "See we are your servants—your slaves."

"Don't be afraid," Joseph said compassionately. "Am I in the place of God? He is the judge, not me. And as for you, you thought evil against me but God meant it for good to save your lives and the lives of our families. Don't be afraid of me. As I promised, I will provide for you and your little ones."

So Joseph and all his father's household lived in Egypt. Joseph died when he was one hundred and ten years old after having seen his great, great grandchildren. His body was embalmed and was put in a coffin in Egypt until the Israelites finally left Egypt about two hundred years later in the time of Moses. Joseph was buried in Shechem near Samaria in the parcel of land given to him by his father Jacob.

You Decide

1. *How do you think Jacob felt toward his sons when he finally heard the whole story of what had happened to Joseph?*

2. *What did Joseph mean when he said, "You thought evil against me, but God meant it for good"?*

2.

A SCEPTER OR A ROD

I

When the Lord said to him, 'Know for certain that your descendants will be strangers in a country not their own, and they will be enslaved and mistreated four hundred years. But I will punish the nation they serve as slaves, and afterward they will come out with great possessions' " (Genesis 15:13-14 NIV).

It was grueling, torturous work under the hot Egyptian sun. Day after day and year after year the Israelites mixed the mud with water, sand, and chopped straw, treaded the mixture for long hours until it was thoroughly blended, and put it into wooden molds to dry, always under the stern eyes of the merciless Egyptian taskmasters. Any slack in pace meant a cruel whip across the back. Any rebellion meant death.

Even under this great affliction the Israelites seemed to grow stronger physically and numerically until they began to outnumber the Egyptians.

"The people of Israel are more and mightier than we," declared the king of Egypt in alarm. "If there should be a war, they might join our enemies and fight against us."

Seeing that harder labor and longer hours seemed to strengthen the Israelites, the king determined to reduce their numbers by another means. Calling his leaders to him, the king commanded that all male Hebrew babies be thrown into the river and drowned. Only females were to live.

This was the situation into which Moses was born. But Amram, his father, and Jochebed, his mother, determined to hide their baby boy. Aaron and Miriam, the older children in the family, took their turns holding and rocking the baby. But finally it became impossible to hide him any longer. Jochebed took some reeds and carefully wove them together to make a little ark. She daubed the inside with pitch to make it waterproof. Then she lovingly wrapped her baby in a little blanket and put him into it. Setting it afloat in the bulrushes near the river's bank, she told her daughter Miriam to watch it closely to see what would happen. Jochebed remained a distance away to pray to God for his mercy on her little son.

Soon the daughter of Pharaoh, king of Egypt, came with her maids to the river to bathe. The birds among the reeds were especially noisy that morning but over their songs she thought she heard a little cry. Suddenly she spied the ark and sent one of her maids to get it. As the maid pushed it in the water toward her, Pharaoh's daughter heard the distinct cry of a baby.

"It's one of the Hebrew children," she exclaimed as she opened the lid and saw the baby. "Isn't he beautiful! There, there, don't cry," she said tenderly picking him up. "I have you. No one will harm you. I will take you to be my baby."

Nestled close to Pharaoh's daughter the baby quieted. Then realizing he was not going to be fed, the baby began to whimper again.

"He must be hungry," the princess said.

At that moment Miriam edged her way closer.

"I know a Hebrew woman who can nurse the baby," she said. "Shall I go and call her for you?"

"Yes," said the princess, delighted that this problem would be taken care of so easily.

Miriam of course went and got her mother. Jochebed's heart leaped within her when she saw her baby in the princess' arms but her steps were firm and her voice steady as she offered to nurse the baby.

"Take the child with you for now," said Pharaoh's daughter. "Nurse him as long as he needs it and I will pay you wages. When he is weaned, he will be my child."

Jochebed nodded and received the baby from the princess' arms. It wasn't until she and Miriam were several yards away that she allowed the tears of joy to come. She said, "God has heard and answered my prayer."

The time went by too quickly for Jochebed but finally, when the baby was about three years old, she brought him to Pharaoh's daughter and he became her son as had been agreed.

"I will name him Moses," said Pharaoh's daughter, "because I took him out of the water."

Moses life-style was changed overnight as he was introduced to the palace of Pharaoh and to the courts of luxury. No longer would he wear the rough clothes of the Hebrews but soft white linen and eventually the white loincloth and girdle of Egyptian noblemen. Learning would not be at his father's knee but in the temple school and later at the outstanding university of the day. Moses would learn all the wisdom the Egyptians had to offer plus the military skills necessary for a commander. He would be a prince, mighty in words and deeds.

Years later as Moses moved among the people, his appearance showed the contrast of cultures. In outward manner and appearance he was an Egyptian nobleman. His skin was clean-shaven and scented with expensive oils and perfumes. He wore the fine white linen tunic and jeweled collar of a royal prince. His rough features, however, though commanding, were not those of a highborn Egyptian. Moses pondered this and occasionally let his mind search out and dwell on the lives of the Hebrew slaves.

One day as Moses went out to inspect the slaves as was his duty, he, for the first time, clearly understood their burdens. He watched, horrified as an Egyptian taskmaster mercilessly beat an old Hebrew slave. Looking around carefully and seeing no one near, he gave in to his anger and killed the Egyptian. Then, in panic, he hastily buried him in the sand.

The next day he returned to the brickyards. As he approached the mud troughs he saw two Hebrews in a violent quarrel. Instinctively he tried to separate them.

"Who made you a prince and judge over us?" the aggressor said. "Are you going to kill me like you killed the Egyptian yesterday?"

Shocked, Moses realized that his deed was known. Had the Egyptians found out too? He knew their punishment for traitors. Fearfully he fled to the land of Midian in the desert and none too soon. When Pharaoh heard of this deed, he searched for him to kill him.

You Decide

1. Do you think Jochebed made a wise decision to let her son be reared by an

Egyptian even though she knew the Egyptians did not worship God?

2. How did she show her trust in God to take care of her baby?

3. Why do you think Moses was drawn to the plight of the Hebrew slaves?

4. If you were Moses escaping from Egypt, how would you feel?

II

Tired and hungry, his skin scorched by the desert sun and his hair matted with sweat and dust, Moses rested beside a well in Midian. All he had learned in Egypt seemed useless here in the desert. Every step he had taken seemed to scream, "failure, failure." What did life hold for him here? What did life hold for him anywhere?

As he sat at the well seven young girls, the daughters of Jethro, a Midianite priest, came up to the well to water their father's sheep. The girls drew up the water in goatskin bags and poured it into nearby troughs where the sheep could drink. Before they had finished watering their animals, a band of shepherds appeared with goats and drove the girls' flock away from the well. Moses quickly leaped to his feet and taking a stick, chased the shepherds and their animals away. Then he helped the girls gather their scattered sheep together and waited as they finished watering them.

When the girls arrived home, they told their father what Moses had done.

"And where is he?" asked Jethro. "Why haven't you brought him with you? Call him so he can eat with us."

Moses willingly accepted the priest's invitation. Here in this home Moses found a peace he had not known and soon agreed to live with Jethro and his family. Jethro taught Moses how to care for his flocks. There was much to learn to become a good shepherd: how to survive in these new surroundings, how to find pasture land, and how to find water and food in unlikely places. In future years this valuable knowledge would save Moses' life and the lives of the Israelites.

In time Moses married Jethro's daughter Zipporah and she bore him two sons, Gershom and Eliezer. Finding contentment in his new home and surroundings, Moses worked for forty years as a shepherd. At first he refused to let even the smallest thought of Egypt enter his mind. But little by little the cries from Egypt's brickyards seemed to mingle with the bleating of the sheep.

One day as Moses was keeping the flock, he led them to the mountain of God, Mount Sinai. Looking up to the sharp crags above, he saw a strange sight. There on the side of a rocky ledge was a bush burning, but it was not being consumed by the fire. Moses went closer to see how this could be.

"Moses, Moses," a voice called out.

Moses looked behind him, sure that whoever was speaking was very close.

"Here I am," he answered.

"Do not come near," the voice continued from the bush. "Take off your shoes, Moses, for you are standing on holy ground. I am the God of your father, the God of Abraham, the God of Isaac, and the God of Jacob."

Moses hid his face with his arms. He knew this was the voice of God, the one they said was above all gods and he was afraid to look.

"I have seen my people oppressed in Egypt under cruel taskmasters. I have heard their cries and I know their sorrows. I have come to deliver them out of the power of the Egyptians and to bring them into a good land of their own."

Moses hungered to hear more but he couldn't comprehend what God said next.

"I will send you to Pharaoh. I will use you to bring my people out of Egypt."

Moses' empathy for the Israelites had grown during his time in the desert, but past experience now told him he was not the man for the job. Forty years earlier he had tried to rescue a Hebrew from an Egyptian. That had resulted in a murder from which his conscience had never fully recovered. He had tried to reconcile two quarreling Hebrews but his efforts had not been appreciated. His motives had been misjudged. How could he possibly go back?

"Who am I that I should go to Pharaoh? Who am I that I should bring your people out of Egypt?" Moses questioned.

"I will go with you," answered God, "and when you have brought them out, you are to bring them to this mountain to serve me."

"But when I go to them and tell them the God of their fathers has sent me," Moses continued, "they'll say, 'How do you know him? What is his name?' What shall I tell them?"

God said to Moses, "I AM THAT I AM. Tell them that I AM has sent you."

Then Moses understood that the creator God who had existed from eternity was speaking to him. He knelt with his face to the ground and worshiped him.

"The elders of my people will believe you, Moses. You and the elders shall go to the king of Egypt and tell him that I have met with you. You will ask him to let you go three days' journey into the wilderness to sacrifice to me. He will not let you go unless he is forced to do so. Therefore I will stretch out my hand and strike Egypt with wonders. After that he will let you go. And when you leave, the Egyptians will give you silver, jewels, and clothes to take with you."

But Moses was hardly listening.

"They won't believe me," he argued. "They will say you haven't really appeared to me."

Then God gave Moses two miraculous signs of his power to show to the Israelites and to

Pharaoh. He commanded Moses to throw his shepherd's rod to the ground. Moses did so and the rod became a live snake. God then commanded Moses to take hold of the snake by its tail. Moses cautiously obeyed and the snake turned back into a rod. Then God told Moses to put his hand into his robe. Once again Moses did as God said but his hand became leprous. Horrified, Moses thrust his hand back into his robe and it returned to normal.

"But I am not eloquent," Moses further protested. "I can neither speak well nor persuasively."

"Who made your mouth, Moses?" God admonished. "I know what you can do. I will be with you and I will teach you what to say."

In despair Moses pleaded with God to get a substitute. God finally allowed Aaron, Moses' brother, to go with him as his spokesman; however, this divided command later caused problems. God didn't need Aaron for the job of delivering the children of Israel. All he needed was Moses.

When God had finished talking with Moses, Moses returned to Jethro. Telling his father-in-law all that had happened, Moses asked permission to go back to his relatives in Egypt.

"Go in peace," Jethro said.

Moses took his wife and sons and set them on donkeys and began his return to the land of Egypt.

Meanwhile God spoke to Aaron in Egypt and told him to go out to meet Moses. Unlike Moses, Aaron didn't yet know God's plan, only that he must find his brother. Heading in the direction of Midian, he met Moses and embraced him and kissed him. Moses told Aaron all that God had told him and Aaron confirmed God's guidance.

Together they went to gather the Israelite elders. Aaron was Moses' spokesman to the elders and Moses showed God's signs of proof. When the people heard that God knew of their affliction and would free them from slavery, they bowed their heads and worshiped.

You Decide

1. *Why do you think God didn't use Moses to rescue his people while Moses was in Egypt? Why would he send him to Midian for forty years?*

2. *What spiritual qualities did Moses need to develop for such a task?*

3. *How would it help Moses to know how the king of Egypt would react?*

4. *Do you think Moses' brother, Aaron, would be a good link between Moses, who was reared an Egyptian, and the Israelites? Why?/Why not?*

5. *Why would it be hard for you to go back into a situation where you'd experienced failure?*

III

Forty years earlier, Moses had walked freely into Pharaoh's court as an Egyptian. Now he was a Hebrew representing God and petitioning for an audience with the Pharaoh. The request was granted and Moses and Aaron entered a long, high-ceilinged room which was lined with thick granite columns. The walls were painted with brightly colored murals and at the far end of the room, seated on a throne raised high by marble steps, sat Pharaoh, king of Egypt. His very appearance was intimidating. He was dressed in sheer white linen and wearing the high red and white crown of Egypt. A heavy jeweled collar hung around his neck, and his arms and fingers were wrapped in brilliant bracelets and rings. Golden slippers adorned his feet, and he held a golden scepter in his hand.

Surrounding Pharaoh were bodyguards with their arms folded in attention, court officials and priests in purple robes. Young handmaidens softly waved long feathered fans to cool the air.

"The God of Israel has spoken to us," Aaron announced. "He has said, 'Let my people go a three-day journey into the wilderness to worship me.' "

"Let Israel go?" A contemptuous smile played around Pharaoh's lips. His icy stare matched the tone of his voice. "Who is this

God, that I should obey his voice?" Then his eyes narrowed and he said with a sneer, "I know not this God and neither will I let Israel go."

As Aaron started to persist, Pharaoh cut him off angrily, with a sweep of his hand. "You waste my time. Why do you take the people from their jobs? There is much work to be done and you are causing my workers to become lazy."

Abruptly Pharaoh left Moses and Aaron standing before the empty throne and went straight to the chief taskmaster.

"It appears that the slaves have too much leisure time. From now on they shall produce the same number of bricks as before but they can go out and cut their own straw. I will not have them idle and listening to lies of a three-day journey to go and worship their God."

In Moses' imagination he had not counted on the situation of the slaves becoming worse. He had somehow envisioned them quietly awaiting the time of their deliverance while God dealt with Pharaoh. But now their burdens under the blistering Egyptian sun had suddenly doubled and who could they blame but Moses.

The Israelite foremen rushed to Pharaoh crying, "Why are you doing this? We cannot make the same number of bricks when we have to go out and gather straw too. The taskmasters are beating us when we are powerless to comply"

"You are lazy," Pharaoh answered coolly. "You are not working hard enough. Obviously if you want to go out and worship your God you have too much time to think." Then he added, "Get back to work and give me my full quota of bricks."

When Moses and Aaron came to the foremen, the Israelites turned their backs on them.

"You have not helped us," they cried. "You have only made us offensive in Pharaoh's eyes."

Moses prayed to God. "Why have you brought evil on your people, God? Why did you even send me here? Pharaoh has made their plight far worse than it was before I came. He hasn't let them go."

God repeated his promise to Moses and said that not only would Pharaoh eventually let the people go, but he would actually drive them out. God promised to rescue the Israelites and to take them for his own people and to bring them into the land he had promised to Abraham, Isaac, and Jacob.

After being assured by God, Moses told this to the children of Israel, but still they would not listen because of their burdens.

Then God told Moses to go to Pharaoh. Reluctant to go back, Moses argued that if the Israelites wouldn't listen to him, neither would Pharaoh.

This time when Moses and Aaron appeared before him, Pharaoh demanded that they perform miracles to demonstrate the power of their God.

At Moses' command Aaron threw his rod before Pharaoh and it became a snake. But Pharaoh called to his wise men and magicians. They too threw down their rods and the rods became snakes. Startled, Moses and Aaron stepped backward but then watched in amazement as Aaron's snake ate the other snakes. This should have impressed Pharaoh but he simply dismissed it as trickery.

The next morning God told Moses to go out to the river bank and meet Pharaoh as he came to the river for water.

"Tell Pharaoh to let my people go to the wilderness to worship me. If he will not let them go, then tell Aaron to stretch his rod over the waters of Egypt and the waters will become blood. By this Pharaoh will know I am God."

As God had predicted, Pharaoh would not let the people go, so Aaron stretched his rod over the water. At once, not only the waters of the Nile River, but the water in the ponds and pools and in the containers in the houses turned to blood. Pharaoh's magicians, however, were able to do this too, but they only had the power to contaminate the water, not purify it. Still Pharaoh's heart was stubborn.

Then God told Moses to go again to Pharaoh and tell him to let the people go and if Pharaoh refused to do so, he would bring a plague of frogs on the land. When Pharaoh refused to let the people go, Aaron stretched the rod over the land and frogs were everywhere, even in the beds, the ovens, and the kneading troughs. The people could not walk without stepping on frogs.

Pharaoh's magicians also were able to produce frogs. However, when the magicians could not rid the land of the frogs, Pharaoh sent for Moses and Aaron.

"Call upon your God so he will take away the frogs, and I will let the people go so they can sacrifice to him," Pharaoh bargained.

Taking Pharaoh at his word, Moses did so and God caused the frogs on the land to die. But when God saw that Pharaoh was ungrateful, he sent a plague of gnats to attack not only the dead frogs but also the people and the animals of the land. The people found it hard to concentrate on anything except the itching caused by the gnats.

This time the magicians were not able to produce gnats and told Pharaoh that this was the finger of God. Nonetheless Pharaoh continued his willful stubbornness since the water of the Israelites had also turned to blood and their land too was covered with frogs and their bodies were infested with gnats.

Then God told Moses to get up early in the morning and go to Pharaoh and tell him that unless he let the people go, God would send huge swarms of flies into the land.

"Tell Pharaoh that this time I will put a division between my people and his people," God told Moses.

When Pharaoh again mocked God, God sent the flies. Flies were everywhere biting through human sweat and polluting food.

Quickly Pharaoh sent for Moses and Aaron and tried to work out a compromise.

"You may sacrifice to your God," he said, "but do so here in the land."

"We cannot do that," answered Moses. "Our sacrificing would be an abomination to the Egyptians because they say these animals are sacred. They would stone us. Besides God said we must go a three-day journey into the wilderness to worship him."

Pharaoh tried another compromise.

"I will let you go," he said in a condescending way, "only don't go very far. And," he added, "pray to your God for me."

"I will go," said Moses, "and I will ask God to take away the flies but see to it that you don't deal deceitfully anymore and will let the people go."

Accordingly, Moses went away and asked God to take away the flies. But as Pharaoh saw what he perceived as God relenting, he hardened his heart and refused to let the people go. God brought a very severe disease on all the Egyptian cattle and because Pharaoh refused to grow any wiser, he sent terrible boils on all the people. Still Pharaoh would not listen to Moses. His will had become strong and unchanging.

The seventh plague sent by God was a plague of hail. Since rain was infrequent in Egypt and hail was unknown, God sent warning to the people through Moses to seek shelter for their animals and themselves. Those who believed God did so, but those who did not believe lived their lives as usual.

The thunderous pounding on the rooftops drove the terrified people to crouch together in the corners of their houses. Hour after hour they remained as the hail beat down all the vegetation outside and shattered the limbs of the trees that were laden with fruit. Only in the land of Goshen where the children of Israel lived was there no hail.

This time Pharaoh called to Moses and for the first time acknowledged his sin. However, his heart was still hardened, and he would not let the people go into the wilderness. So God sent a tribe of locusts to consume the seed that was not hurt by the hail. All hopes of a harvest were entirely lost.

Pharaoh again tried to get Moses to compromise, saying the men could go but that they should leave their children and wives behind them as a pledge of their return. Moses again would not compromise God's command.

Then God told Moses to stretch his hand toward heaven. At once a thick darkness covered Egypt, so dark the Egyptians could not see one another. Blindly they groped to find their way, and those at home didn't leave their houses for three days. But the children of Israel had light in their houses.

Seemingly defeated, Pharaoh called Moses and made his last proposal for compromise.

"Go and worship your God," he said. "You may take your children with you but leave your animals."

"We must take the animals," Moses insisted. "We won't know what to sacrifice to God until we get there."

"Get out," Pharaoh shouted angrily, jumping to his feet. "Don't let me see your face again, for if I do you will surely die."

"Well spoken," said Moses. "I will see your face no more."

You Decide

1. What basic human characteristic did Pharaoh display before God?

2. What basic human characteristic did Moses display before God?

3. What three compromises did Pharaoh try to make with Moses?

4. What information did Moses have from God that would help him resist the temptation to compromise?

IV

God brought one final plague on the Egyptians. This was the death of all firstborns in the land from the firstborn of Pharaoh to the firstborn of the lowest servant and even including the firstborn of the livestock. The Egyptians believed that the firstborn belonged to the gods of Egypt. Now God was going to show them his power over all the Egyptian gods.

God gave his people explicit instructions. First, they were to ask their Egyptian neighbors for jewels of silver and of gold. The Egyptians willingly gave to the Israelites, some in order to hasten their departure and others because they had become neighbors and friends.

"Each family is to kill a lamb and put its blood on the two doorposts and the lintel of their house," God commanded. "When the death angel comes, he will pass over the houses where he sees the blood of the lamb. But in the houses where there is no blood, the firstborn will die."

If any Egyptian believed this and he too put blood on his doorposts, his house would be passed over by the death angel. All that was necessary was belief in what God said.

The family was also to roast the lamb and eat it with unleavened bread and bitter herbs and be ready to leave at a moment's notice.

At midnight the usual quiet darkness was broken by the first sound of wailing. Soon there was other wailing until it was as if the whole land itself were moaning as all of the firstborn of the Egyptians died. Cattle lay dead in the pastures. And in the palace, the firstborn son of Pharaoh died. Great was the cry in Egypt as Pharaoh rose up in the night with all his servants.

When Moses and Aaron arrived at the palace in answer to Pharaoh's summons, they found an utterly defeated man, his head in his hands.

"Get out from among my people," Pharaoh said, looking up at them blankly. "Take the people and their flocks and herds and be gone."

The Egyptians also were insistent that the Israelites leave immediately for they did not know where God's judgment would end.

The children of Israel left on foot with all their possessions. By count there were 600,000 men of an age fit for war plus women and children. They had come into Egypt 430 years earlier as Jacob's household of seventy. Now they were leaving as a people of nearly 3,000,000. They began the hard trek slowly, but they wanted to get as far from Egypt as they could in a short time. Suddenly there appeared before them a pillar of fire. Not hindering their progress, it actually seemed to be guiding them in the darkness. By morning it had changed to a pillar of cloud that was leading them farther from Egypt.

The quickest way for God to lead the Israelites to the promised land was up the seacoast. But that land was occupied by the Philistines. The Israelites had just come out of slavery and had no weapons. They were not prepared for warfare. God took them through the wilderness of the Red Sea, a longer route, but one where they would not yet encounter enemies.

As they camped at the edge of the wilderness by the Red Sea, God spoke to Moses. "Pharaoh will think you are trapped now. His hardened heart will once again make him want to pursue you, but I will show the Egyptians that I am God."

Pharaoh meanwhile called his servants together. "It was a mistake to let those Hebrew slaves go," he lamented.

"It isn't too late," said a counselor. "The route they have taken will lead them into a trap."

"Excellent," exclaimed Pharaoh. "We'll strike at once. The slaves will soon be back at work making more bricks than before."

Pharaoh hastily readied more than 600 chariots, pursued the children of Israel, and overtook them as they were camped by the Red Sea.

The next morning the Israelites, awakened by a cry from the guards, saw the clouds of dust from the Egyptians coming toward them.

"Why have you brought us into the wilderness only to die?" they screamed at Moses. "It would have been better for us to serve the Egyptians than to die in the wilderness."

"Don't be afraid," shouted Moses. "Stand still and see God's salvation which he will show you today. He will fight for you. You will never see the Egyptians again."

The Israelites watched as the pillar of cloud before them moved back and stood between them and the approaching Egyptians so they could not see one another.

"Tell the children of Israel to go forward," God told Moses. "Lift up your rod and stretch it out over the sea and divide it. My people shall cross over it on dry land. But I will harden the stubborn hearts of the Egyptians and they will follow you. Then I will show the Egyptians once and for all that I am God."

Moses turned to the sea and stretched out his rod over it. Immediately God caused the sea to be divided so there was a wall of water on each side of the division. The children of Israel, slowly at first and then with great haste, went into the midst of the sea on dry ground. The cloud remained stationary until the Israelites had crossed safely. When it lifted, the Egyptians pursued them into the sea. When they were about halfway through, sand began to clog the wheels of their chariots.

"Let's go back," the Egyptians cried in terror, "for their God fights for them."

God spoke to Moses on the other side of the Red Sea and said, "Stretch out your hand over the sea again so that the waters may come upon the Egyptians and their chariots."

Moses did so and the sea came together with a torrent, covering the chariots and the whole Egyptian army. Not one of them remained. Therefore, the Israelites feared God and believed his servant Moses.

Happy and finally free, they began to sing and dance.

"God is my strength and song and he has become my salvation," they sang.

You Decide

1. *When the Israelites were afraid they had been trapped by the Red Sea and would be killed by the Egyptians, what previous acts of God in their behalf could they have remembered to help strengthen their faith?*

2. *When we ask for God's help in a situation, why do we sometimes see circumstances get worse before they get better?*

3. *Imagine and describe your feelings when walking between two walls of water.*

V

As the people proceeded into the wilderness of Shur, the reality of the desert set in. An occasional tamarisk tree or acacia bush were about the only plants able to survive in that harsh climate. As far as they could see, the parched desert seemed endless.

"We're thirsty," they began to complain. "Our water has run out and there is no water in sight."

As they fixed their minds on their present problem, they were hindered from remembering what God had done for them only a few days before. Finally, they reached the oasis of Marah, and they ran to the water only to discover that it was so bitter they could not drink it.

"What are we going to do?" the people cried. "We cannot drink this. Why have you brought us here?"

Moses at once prayed to God. After all, he and the people had followed the cloud to Marah. God showed Moses that this was part of the plan to teach the Israelites to trust God. He told Moses to take a nearby tree and throw it into the water whereupon the water became sweet and the people drank. Then with renewed strength, the people continued their journey across the hot sands. Their thoughts turned to the homeland God had promised them. They dreamed of green fields, fresh streams, and great flocks. They looked around them again and saw only the desert. Gradually the supply of food they had brought with them ran out, and as they got hungrier they remembered the plentiful foods of Egypt. They forgot that God had cared for them when they were thirsty. Grumbling bitterly, they went to Moses and Aaron.

"Look, our food is gone. How can we feed our children? Have you brought us out here in the wilderness to starve us to death?"

Again Moses went to God in prayer. In answer, God said bread would rain from heaven. God would not only feed the people but would also test their obedience. God gave precise instructions to the people. Each morning they were to go out and gather their food for the day. On the sixth day they were to gather enough for two days so that they could rest on the seventh day. They were not to gather more than God said or try to store any until the next day. Furthermore, God said he would provide meat for them. By this they would know he was their God.

That evening quail came up and covered the camp.

"There is food enough for everyone," cried the people. "Moses was right. God sent the quail to feed us."

Early the next morning the people arose to find what appeared to be ice particles on the ground.

"What is this?" they asked.

"This is the bread that God has given you to eat," said Moses.

The people tasted the food and excitedly began to gather their day's supply.

"God has provided for today, but how can I be sure there will be more tomorrow?" some asked among themselves.

"I'd better collect all I can," said others. "I'll put half of it aside for tomorrow. No matter what happens to everyone else, our family will not go hungry."

The next morning, however, they found that what was left over had spoiled and become wormy. The people learned that God was faithful, so they gathered only what they needed for the day. On the sixth day they gathered twice as much and laid up what they didn't use until the next day and it did not spoil.

The people called the food "manna." God commanded the Israelites to keep a container of manna to show future generations the food with which God sustained them on their journey from Egypt to the promised land.

As the people proceeded on their way, they again became thirsty and complained against Moses.

"What shall I do with these people?" Moses cried to God. "They are going to kill me."

"Call the people together," God told him. "I will stand before you upon the rock of Horeb. Strike the rock with your rod and water will come out of it so the people can drink."

Moses did as God said and water gushed from the rock, and the people drank as much as they wanted.

God had provided for the physical needs of the people. Now it was time for God to teach them about his protection. While they were camped at Rephidim, close to their immediate destination of Mount Sinai, the Israelites were unexpectedly attacked by a band of Amalekites who were fierce, seminomadic traders from Northern Sinai. The Israelites had never before been tested in battle, and they were poorly equipped. The men carried simple weapons used by shepherds to protect their flocks. Some had slings, staffs, or crude spears while others had bows and arrows. The Amalekites, on the other hand, had bronze-tipped arrows, spears, and swords.

Quickly Moses appointed Joshua to be in command. Moses told Joshua to choose men to fight the Amalekites.

"I will stand on top of the hill with the rod of God in my hand," he said.

Joshua did as Moses said, and Moses chose Aaron and Hur and went to the top of the hill. While Moses held the rod up in his hand, Israel was victorious, but when he lowered his hand, the Amalekites gained ground. Moses' hands got tired so Aaron and Hur moved a stone for him to sit on. Then they stood on either side of Moses and held up his hands until sundown. Joshua and the Israelites thus defeated the Amalekites.

In thanksgiving to God, Moses built an altar and led his people in prayer. Then, fresh from their first military victory, the Israelites eagerly pushed on.

In the third month after leaving Egypt they came to the wilderness of Sinai and camped at the base of the mountain where God had first spoken to Moses. Moses had brought the people there as God had asked. Now God would make a covenant with the people. Moses commanded the people to get ready to meet with God.

On the morning of the third day, thunder rolled across the sky and lightning flashed. There was the sound of a trumpet. Fearfully huddling together, the people assembled at the foot of the mountain, where God spoke in the thunder and gave them the first part of the law which we know as the Ten Commandments.

God told them that he was to be preeminent in their lives—no one and nothing was to come before him. Knowing that they had lived in a land of idols for over four hundred years, God commanded them not to make any images of any likeness, not to bow down to them or worship them. He told them they were not to take his name lightly as if he hadn't the very power of life or death over them. They were also to remember his sabbath and keep it as a holy day. One day out of seven was to be used to worship God and to thank him for the family and surroundings he had provided. He told the Israelites to honor their parents, thus showing God's care and sovereignty over their lives. God told them not to murder or commit a sexual sin against another person. He told them not to steal but to ask him for what they needed. God told them not to lie to one another or about one another but to deal honestly in all their relationships. He also told them not to be jealous and envious of what others had, but to be content.

The people heard the thunder and saw the lightning. They heard the noise of the trumpet and saw the mountain smoking, and they trembled with fear.

"You speak to us, Moses, and we will listen," they said, "but don't let God talk to us or we will die."

Moses went near the thick darkness, and God told him what to tell the people.

"You have seen that I have talked with you directly from heaven. Therefore, you have no need of other gods."

The people promised to do all that God had commanded.

The next day God called Moses to come up the mountain. He told Moses to bring Joshua part of the way with him. Moses stayed for forty days learning what God wanted him to teach the Israelites.

As the days passed and Moses did not return, the people became concerned. They could not go up to look for Moses and Joshua because God had forbidden them to touch the mountain.

"Maybe Moses isn't coming back," they ventured. "If he doesn't, what will we do?"

Feeling lost without their leader, the people forgot God's commandments and their promise to worship him only.

"Let's ask Aaron to make us a statue that we can worship," someone suggested.

"Yes," agreed another. "We need a god we can see."

The people brought their jewelry to Aaron, and Aaron, thinking he alone might be in charge of this multitude, did what the people asked. He melted the gold and fashioned from it a golden statue of a calf.

"It looks like a god our neighbors worshiped in Egypt," one of the Israelites said excitedly.

Early the next morning the people brought their offerings to the altar before the golden calf. They ate and drank and danced with joy. God, however, was not blind to what was going on. He told Moses that the people had made an idol and were worshiping it. God said he would destroy the Israelites completely because they were an ungrateful and disobedient people. Then he would start over and make a new nation of Moses. But Moses fell to his knees.

"If the Egyptians hear of this," he cried, "they will say you led the people out of Egypt but you couldn't bring them to their promised land."

Moses rapidly descended the mountain, bringing with him stone tablets on which were written the Ten Commandments. Partway down the mountain he met Joshua, who was waiting anxiously.

"Listen, Moses," Joshua cried. "It sounds like war in our camp."

"No," said Moses cupping his ear. "I hear singing, but it is not like joyful singing to God. It is strange sounding."

As they neared the bottom of the mountain, Moses stopped in utter disbelief at what he saw. There in the midst of the camp was the huge golden calf. The people were singing and dancing around the idol the way he had seen the Egyptians do. How could they have so quickly forgotten their promise to God? How could they have turned their backs on him? Who had persuaded them to do this? Where was Aaron? Why hadn't he stopped them?

Utterly nauseated by the sight of their revelry, Moses cried out at them and broke the stone tablets. The sight of Joshua and Moses made the people freeze in their action. Aaron shamefully came forward with his head down, not daring to look Moses in the eye.

"Aaron, where did you get this idol?" Moses demanded.

"When you did not return, the people gave me their gold," Aaron admitted. "I threw it into the fire and out came this golden calf."

At once Moses destroyed the idol, grinding it into a powder and throwing it into a stream.

"Now drink the water, all of you," he commanded. "Let this be a lesson to you. Remember what you have done. I will go back up the mountain and ask God to forgive you."

Once again on the mountain Moses bowed before God.

"O God, please forgive us and don't leave us on our own. We do not know how to govern ourselves or how to fight our enemies. Only you can keep us free from diseases. If you do not go with us, we cannot possibly survive."

God promised Moses he would go before them to the land and drive out the enemies living there.

"Do not be afraid. God has forgiven you," Moses assured the people when he returned. "He has given me plans for a tabernacle of worship. It will be a place where we can worship and offer acceptable sacrifices for our sins. Bring your offerings and we will all work together to make it."

After many months of careful, loving work, the tabernacle was ready and the cloud hovered over it. The most special part of the tabernacle housed a box called the ark. In it the Israelites placed the bowl of manna and the new stone tablets on which were written the Ten Commandments.

Now the Israelites were no longer a mob of fleeing slaves. In the one year since they had left Egypt, they had become a nation with laws, leaders, and a place of worship. As other nations looked on, they saw that this was not an unruly mob, but an orderly people camped around their tabernacle according to their tribes. When they marched, it was also by tribes, following their great God who was leading them with a cloud by day and a pillar of fire by night.

You Decide

1. *Name five miraculous ways God cared for the Israelites on their journey from the Red Sea to Mount Sinai.*

2. *Look for ways God worked in your life this week and write them down in a special notebook.*

3. *Imagine you are Moses. How would your feelings about Aaron have changed from the time you both met with Pharaoh until now?*

VI

In the second month of the second year of their journey, the Israelites began their march again. Moses and Aaron led the procession with the Levites, the priestly tribe, carrying the ark and the disassembled parts of the tabernacle. But it seemed that the people could not travel without grumbling against Moses and ultimately against God.

"God, why have you given me these people? All they do is complain," a weary Moses told God. "Am I to carry them as little babies all the way to the land you promised? I can't do it," he cried. "I'm not able to do this all by myself. I'd rather die."

God in answer told Moses to elect seventy men who could help him so he wouldn't have to bear the burden alone.

After this, rebellion rose from within Moses' own family.

"Why are you always the only one in charge, Moses," Miriam began. "Do you think you are the only one who can speak for God? Didn't God call Aaron to be the high priest?"

Hesitatingly Aaron's eyes met Moses' eyes.

"God didn't make you the dispenser of all our knowledge. I am a prophetess, too," continued Miriam.

God, aware that his chosen leader was once again under attack, called Moses, Aaron, and Miriam to the tabernacle.

"I am the one who chooses prophets. I speak to them in visions and dreams," he told them. "But Moses is different. He is faithful in doing all I tell him and I speak to him face to face. Seeing this, you should be afraid to speak against him for I have chosen him for this very purpose."

Glancing uncertainly at Miriam, Aaron was horrified to discover that she had become leprous. Panic-stricken, he confessed their sin to Moses and asked Moses to pray to God for their sister Miriam. Moses fell on his knees asking God's forgiveness. Though God healed Miriam, he commanded that she remain in shame outside the camp for seven days. The people did not travel again until Miriam was brought back into the camp. Then they journeyed until they came to Kadesh-barnea on the southern border of Canaan.

"This is the land God promised you," Moses told the Israelites. "Go possess it as God has commanded. Don't be afraid or discouraged."

The people could hardly believe that they had at last reached their destination. Fearfully they approached Moses with their own plans. "Let's send men before us to spy out the land," they cautioned. "They can tell us how to enter it and into which cities to go."

Moses appointed leaders from each tribe, twelve in all, as spies. "See how many people are there and if they are strong or weak," he charged them. "Find out what the cities are like and if the people live in tents or fortified surroundings. See if the produce of the land is good and if there is wood. Above all, be of good courage and bring back some of the fruit of the land."

The spies stayed in the land of Canaan for forty days. When they returned, they displayed the excellent fruits they had brought with them and gave an account of the many good things the land afforded.

The people eagerly tasted the fruit and waited for the twelve to tell them more.

"But the people there are strong," the spies said. "They live in large, walled cities. Besides that, we saw giants there. The Amalekites live in the south, the Hittites, the Jebusites, and the Amorites live in the mountains, and the Canaanites live by the sea. We can't possibly take that land. We haven't the strength. In fact, we are nothing more than grasshoppers in their sight."

Dismayed and sobered by the news, the people stepped back and began murmuring to one another in small groups. Caleb, one of the spies, rose before Moses and all the congregation of Israel and tried to quiet the people.

"Let us go up at once and possess it," he said. "We are well able to overcome it."

The people's initial joy, however, had turned to confusion and disappointment, and they began to weep and murmur against Moses and Aaron.

"Would to God that we had died in Egypt or even in the wilderness," they lamented. "Why has God brought us to this land? Is it to be killed or that our wives and children should be killed? It would be better if we returned to Egypt."

All night the people cried. By the next morning they had decided they couldn't go ahead. As the cry went up to choose a captain and return to Egypt, Moses and Aaron fell on their faces before God, and Joshua and Caleb tore their clothes in sorrow.

"The land we searched out is an exceedingly good land," Joshua and Caleb shouted over the cries of the people. "If God delights in us, he will give it to us. Don't rebel against him and don't fear the people of Canaan. God is with us."

One by one the people began to gather stones to throw at them.

God was very angry. "How long will these people provoke me by their unbelief? Because they refuse to believe, even after seeing my glory and the miracles that I have done, and they will not follow my leading, they will never enter the land I promised to their forefathers. They will wander in this wilderness one year for each day the spies were in the land, forty years in all. All those twenty years old and older will die in the wilderness except Joshua and Caleb. I will bring into the land the children who they are so sure will be killed in it. The children will have the land that their parents despise."

Upon hearing this, the people returned to their tents mourning greatly. By the next morning they had decided that going into the land really would be better than wandering in the wilderness for forty more years.

"We have sinned," they confessed. "We will go up and take the land God promised to us."

But it was too late and Moses pleaded with them not to go.

"God will not go with you," he warned.

The people, however, stubbornly refused to believe God's judgment was final. They organized a band of men and went into the hills to fight. Quickly the Amalekites and the Canaanites who lived there came down and beat them back. Those who were not killed fled in shame back to their camp.

You Decide

1. *All twelve spies came back with the same information. What accounted for the differences in their interpretation of these facts?*

2. *What logical argument could Moses have used against sending spies into the land before all the people went?*

3. *Has God ever asked you to act on faith rather than on logical determination?*

VII

Facing the fact that it would be forty more years of desert traveling and living, the Israelites began a period of aimlessness and discontent. Still Moses led them faithfully, always trying to help them learn from their mistakes. Time and time again the leadership became jealous of Moses' and Aaron's authority. But God consistently reaffirmed Moses' position as leader and Aaron as high priest.

After wandering about thirty-seven years, the people again came to Kadesh where they had refused to go into the promised land. There Miriam died and was buried.

Maybe it was the old surroundings that prompted the people to begin grumbling again. "Why have you brought us into this wilderness to die? There is no seed here, no figs, no vines, no pomegranates. There isn't even any water."

Moses and Aaron, as was their habit, took the matter before God.

"Gather the people together and *speak* to the rock before their eyes," God said. "The rock will give forth water for the people and their animals."

Moses called the people together and took Aaron's rod, and after having deliberately asked for God's specific instructions, this time he failed to follow them.

"Here now, you rebels," he chided, "must we fetch water for you out of this rock?"

With that he lifted the rod and *struck* the rock twice, and water came out and the people and the animals drank.

God spoke to Moses and Aaron, confronting them with their disobedience. "Because you didn't believe and obey me and because you took credit for providing water for the people, you will not bring this congregation into the land I have given them."

Slowly, the Israelites approached the promised land, this time from the east. As they approached Mount Hor, God told Moses to take Aaron and Eleazar, Aaron's son, up to the mount. There Moses took Aaron's priestly garments and put them on Eleazar. Aaron died there on top of the mountain and all of the people mourned for him for thirty days. Then Eleazar became their high priest.

Within sight of the promised land, Moses begged God to allow him to continue as leader and to go over and see the good land beyond the Jordan River. But God was firm with Moses for the sake of the children of Israel.

"That is enough," he said. "Don't speak to me any more about this matter. Go up to the top of Mount Nebo and look westward and northward and southward and eastward and see the land with your eyes. You shall not go over, but commission Joshua, encourage and strengthen him, for he shall lead the people. He will cause them to inherit the land which you shall see."

So Moses took Joshua before Eleazar, the priest, and said to him in the sight of all Israel, "Be strong, courageous, and firm, for you shall go with these people to the land that God promised their fathers, and you shall cause them to possess it. God will go before you. Don't flinch or be afraid. Don't become depressed or dismayed for God will not fail you or let you go."

Then turning to the people, Moses said: "What other nation has God been so close to as he is to us so that he answers all their needs? What other nation has laws and judgments as righteous as those given by God? When you are settled in the land don't forget to teach your sons and daughters what you have seen and heard. Tell them the Lord your God led you these forty years in the wilderness to humble you and to test you, to know what was in your heart, whether you would keep his commandments or not. He let you hunger and he fed you with manna, which neither you nor your fathers had ever seen. Your clothes did not wear out, neither did your feet swell these forty years. Remember these things when you get to the land of plenty and remember that it is God who gives them to you. Don't say in your heart, 'My power and my might have gotten me this wealth.' Love your God. Obey his voice and cling to him so you may live in the land that he promised to give to your fathers, to Abraham, to Isaac, and to Jacob.

"Today I am one hundred twenty years old and God has said to me, 'You shall not go over this Jordan.' But Joshua shall go over before you as God has said."

Then Moses went up to the top of Mount Nebo and God showed him all the land that he had promised to the Israelites. And Moses, the servant of God, died there in the land of Moab as God had said.

"Since then no prophet has risen in Israel like Moses, whom the Lord knew face to face, who did all those miraculous signs and wonders the Lord sent him to do in Egypt—to Pharaoh and to all his officials and to his whole land. For no one has ever shown the mighty power or performed the awesome deeds that Moses did in the sight of all Israel" (Deuteronomy 34:10-12 NIV).

You Decide

1. *Do you think God was fair when he refused to let Moses lead the Israelites into the promised land? Why?/Why not?*

2. *Why was it so important that Moses obey God's instructions in this particular event?*

3. *Did Moses ever get to go to the promised land? (Read Matthew 17:1-8; Mark 9:2-8; Luke 9:28-36.)*

3.

TWICE A GIFT

I

Samuel was born into a unique family. His father, Elkanah, had two wives. Peninnah, one of the wives, had children but Hannah, the other wife, had none.

"Poor Hannah," Peninnah mocked. "What a disgrace not to be able to bear her husband even one child. God has surely favored me for I have given Elkanah both sons and daughters."

Whenever Elkanah sacrificed to God, he gave Peninnah and her children portions of the sacrificial meat. He gave Hannah, however, a double portion because he loved her even though she had no children.

Each year the family went up to the temple and each time Peninnah taunted Hannah because she had no children. Hannah cried and would not eat.

"Why are you crying?" Elkanah asked. "Am I not worth more to you than ten sons?"

But Hannah went into the temple and prayed to God.

"O God," she cried, "if you will give me a son I will dedicate him to you and give him to you as long as he lives."

Many parents pray for their children, and they dedicate them to God. Few, however, give them physically to the Lord. This is what Hannah did. God answered her prayer and she had a son and named him Samuel which means "heard of God."

Hannah then stayed at home with Samuel and did not go back to the temple to sacrifice until Samuel was weaned, which in those days meant he was three to five years old. This was the time she had chosen to give him to God. It must have been very difficult for Hannah to leave Samuel with the priest at the temple even though she had undoubtedly prepared him for this. Samuel too must have been quite homesick for his family. However, there were women who worked in the temple service who probably cared for him. Hannah knew that it was important for Samuel to be trained there from his early boyhood so his earliest impressions would be those of the temple of God. We never hear about Samuel having any resentment toward his family, but we do know that he loved and served God throughout his whole life.

At the temple, Samuel came in contact with a variety of influences. Eli, though a priest of God and a representative to the people, was not always the good example a priest should be. His two grown sons who were priests at Shiloh were evil and worthless. They didn't know God and didn't care to know him. Eli knew his sons cheated by taking more than priests were allowed to take from the people who brought sacrifices to the temple. He also knew they led immoral lives with the women who served in the temple, yet he didn't restrain them from being priests.

"Why do you do such things?" Eli asked. "I hear of your evil dealings from all the people. They are telling everyone. Don't you know you're not only wronging the people, but that you're sinning against God?"

His sons would not listen to their father.

Finally, God sent a prophet to Eli with a message for him. "God says," the man told Eli, " 'I chose your forefathers to be priests before me, but now by your actions you show that you despise my sacrifice and offerings. You honor your sons above me by fattening yourselves upon the choicest parts of every offering my people bring. Therefore, the time is coming when I will cut off the strength of your house.

There will not be an old man in your family. They will all die in their best years.' "

Then the man gave Eli a way to prove that what he said was true.

"What happens to your two sons shall be a sign to you: in one day they will both die."

While Samuel lived at the temple, Eli was his principal teacher. What a contrast Samuel was to Eli's own sons. He obediently learned what it meant to love and worship God. While Eli's sons were rejecting God and disgusting the people, the little boy, Samuel, performed his temple duties before God and pleased God and the people.

Probably Hannah didn't know all of this when she took Samuel to the temple to live. She did trust God, and she knew he had answered her prayer by giving her this child.

Each year Samuel's mother made him a little robe and brought it to him when the family came to the temple to worship. Each year Samuel eagerly looked forward to the visit and to getting the robe which he kept, knowing that his mother cared about him. Even though his parents eventually had three other sons and two daughters whom they brought and introduced to Samuel, they prayed for Samuel as their special son who was serving God.

You Decide

1. Have you ever vowed to do something for God if he would answer your prayer?

2. *What place do parents have in teaching their children to obey God's authority?*

3. *Explain: "You are the only Bible some of your friends will ever read."*

4. *What influence for good does your family have on you? Your friends? Your school?*

II

One evening, after Samuel had lived in the temple several years, he was awakened in the night by a voice calling, "Samuel."

"Here I am," he answered as he ran to Eli to see what he wanted.

"I did not call you," said Eli sleepily. "Go back to bed."

Samuel went back to lay down. Again he heard someone call softly but very distinctly, "Samuel."

Samuel went again to Eli and said, "Here I am for you called me."

"I did not call you, my son," Eli yawned. "Lie down again."

Even though Samuel was working in the temple he did not know that God could relate in a personal way to him. He did not know it was the voice of God calling him.

"Samuel," the voice came again the third time. Samuel again got up and went to Eli.

"Here I am for you did call me."

Then Eli understood that it was God who was calling Samuel, and he said, "Go, lie down, and if he calls you again, say to him, 'Speak, God, for your servant is listening.'"

Samuel went and lay down again as before. God came and called, "Samuel, Samuel." Samuel answered as Eli had told him.

"Speak, God, for your servant is listening."

Then God told Samuel a startling thing: "I am going to do to Eli all I warned him I would do," he said. "I will judge and punish his house forever because his sons spoke with contempt against me and he did nothing about it."

Imagine how Samuel must have felt. He lay there wide awake. God had spoken to him. Samuel had learned that God was all-wise and all-knowing and that he didn't make mistakes. If Samuel had seen Eli ignore his sons' behavior, surely God had seen too. Why hadn't Eli stopped his sons? Samuel didn't want Eli to be punished. Yet he knew that God would be true to his word. Samuel wanted God to be merciful and loving to Eli, but he knew God couldn't be really merciful and loving if he were not also righteous and just. Then Samuel remembered that God is also forgiving and will always forgive a truly repentant person.

Samuel slept restlessly until morning finally came. As the sun streamed in through his window, Samuel reluctantly got up. He went about his usual routine of opening the doors of the temple but he didn't go to Eli.

"God, how can I face Eli?" he said. "Must I be the one to tell him what you said?"

Eli, however, called Samuel. When Samuel answered and went to him, Eli questioned him as to what God had said.

"What did he tell you? Do not hide it from me. May God do to you all he said if you don't tell me everything."

Samuel told all that God had said, hiding nothing.

"It is from God." Eli's voice was somber and barely audible. "Let him do what seems good to him."

Eli had apparently given up. He still could not bear to expel his sons from the priesthood.

You Decide

1. *How does God make himself known to people?*

2. *What would a positive response to God be? A negative response?*

3. *Was Samuel honest when he told Eli what the Lord had said?*

4. *How do you feel about Eli's response to what Samuel told him?*

III

As the years went by, Samuel continued to grow physically and to grow in his relationship to God. God was with him and helped him speak wisely so that everyone knew God had chosen him to be a prophet.

During Samuel's lifetime, the Israelites were often at war with their Philistine neighbors. God had given the Israelites this land and had always helped them in their battles to preserve it. One particular time, however, about four thousand Israelites were killed in battle.

"Why has God let the Philistines defeat us today?" cried the people. Then someone had an idea.

"Let's carry the ark of the covenant of God into battle with us. That way God will be with us and spare us from our enemies."

The ark was a very special piece of furniture used in the tabernacle. It had been built according to the exact specifications given by God, and it contained such special objects as the bowl of manna and the stone tablets on which were written the Ten Commandments. It was only a piece of furniture. It reminded the Israelites of God's law and provision for them but it did not contain God. The people were not crying to God for help. They were relying on superstition and a mere object to help them. But Eli's sons thought this was a good idea, and they took the ark to the battlefield. All the people cheered.

The Philistines were alarmed by the sight of Israel bringing the ark into battle, but they determined to fight harder against Israel.

"We have gods, too," they concluded, "and perhaps ours are stronger."

This time as the battle raged there was a great slaughter and thirty thousand Israelites died. The Philistines captured the ark of God and killed both of Eli's sons. One man escaped and ran to Eli, who was now an old, blind man.

"What is it?" Eli called out as he heard the runner.

"I have come from the battle," the man gasped.

"Tell me. How did the battle go?" Eli asked anxiously.

"Many Israelites were killed and the rest fled from the Philistines," he panted. "Your two sons are among the dead and the Philistines have captured the ark of God."

At the mention of the ark, Eli fell backward off his seat and broke his neck, and died.

Samuel now replaced Eli and led the people back to a true worship of God. Every year he went from place to place throughout Israel to act as a judge. Then he would return to his home in Ramah.

When Samuel was old he made his own sons judges in Israel. But his sons were not like Samuel. They took bribes and they perverted justice. The elders of Israel went to Samuel to complain.

"We don't want your sons to be our judges anymore. We want you to appoint a king like all the other nations have," they said.

Samuel fell on his knees before God, burying his face in his hands.

"O God," he cried, "where have I failed to make your way clear so that these, your people, would choose such a path? They want to be like the nations around them, not different, not uniquely chosen, but like all the heathen nations."

"Do what they say, Samuel," God said, comforting him. "They are not rejecting you, they are rejecting me. They do not trust me to be their king. Do what they say, only warn them of what an earthly king who reigns over them will do."

Samuel gathered the people and told them all that God had said. "These are the things a king who reigns over you will demand," Samuel warned. "He will take your sons and appoint them to be his horsemen and to run before his chariots. He will appoint them to be his commanders, to plow his ground, to reap his harvest, and to make his weapons. He will take your daughters to be perfumers, cooks, and bakers. He will take the best of your fields, vineyards, and olive orchards and give them to his servants. He will take a tenth of your produce to give to his servants. He will take your servants, the best of your cattle and donkeys and use them in his work. He will take a tenth of your flocks. You will be slaves to your king. When you call to God and complain about this king you have chosen, he will not hear you."

The people refused to heed Samuel's warning. "No," they said resolutely, "we want a king to reign over us. We want him to go out before us and fight our battles."

God selected Samuel to anoint Israel's first king. Samuel didn't know who this king would be, but he trusted God to lead him to the man. The man chosen by God was Saul. Saul was a modest and handsome young man. He was also a head taller than all the people. God revealed to Samuel that the man he would send to him would be from the tribe of Benjamin. He was to anoint this man as king.

One day Saul was on an errand to find his father's donkeys which had strayed. Because Samuel was a man of God, Saul went to him to inquire where the donkeys might be. Samuel told him that the donkeys had already been found and returned to his father. Then, knowing that Saul was a Benjamite, he invited him and his servant to eat with him and spend the night in his house before returning home.

The next day Samuel took a vial of oil and anointed Saul and told him God had chosen him to be king over Israel. He told Saul that the Spirit of God would come on him to confirm this anointing. Saul could then be used by God to lead his people. If he were obedient to God, he could know God's wisdom and judgment and have an intimate relationship with God just as Samuel did.

Saul returned home and was met by his uncle.

"Where did you go?" Saul's uncle asked.

"To find the donkeys," Saul answered, "but when I couldn't find them I went to Samuel."

"What did Samuel say to you?" asked his uncle.

"He told me the donkeys had been found," said Saul, but he didn't tell his uncle anything about the kingship.

A short time later, Samuel called all the people together for a meeting at Mizpah. "God is the one who brought you out of Egypt and delivered you from all your enemies," he said. "But now you have rejected him by saying you want a king. So line up and present yourselves before him by tribes so he can show you who your chosen king will be."

As the tribes advanced, the tribe of Benjamin was selected. As the families of the tribe of Benjamin were presented, Saul's family was singled out. Last of all, Saul was chosen from his family, but when they looked for him they could not find him. He had hidden.

When Samuel finally introduced him to the people, he said, "See the man God has chosen. There is none other like him."

"Long live the king," all the people shouted.

Since there had not been a king before, Samuel wrote in a book how this king should rule the nation. He wrote of the king's relationship to God and of his relationship to the people. This was a time of transition for the nation of Israel. No longer would they be ruled by judges, but by their king. Samuel, however, continued as God's prophet. He also offered the sacrifices for the nation to God. Samuel gave wise counsel to Saul and loved him as a close, personal friend.

You Decide

1. *What happened to cause the Israelites to want a king?*
2. *Why do you think the Israelites didn't choose Samuel to lead them?*
3. *What are the dangers of choosing to be like all your friends?*
4. *Did God allow the Israelites to follow their choice to have a king?*
5. *Will he allow you to be like your friends if this is your choice? Why?*

IV

Not long after Saul was proclaimed king, the Ammonites, Israel's neighbors to the east, attacked the Israelites who lived in Jabesh-gilead. The Israelites tried to make a treaty with their attackers instead of fighting to defend the land God had given them, but the Ammonite commander determined to set the terms.

"I'll only make a treaty with you on one condition: I will put out the right eyes of all your men and thereby disgrace all Israel."

When the Israelites fought with swords or spears, they held up shields in front of them with their left hands. They peeked over the top-right sides with their right eyes and thrust their swords at the enemy with their right hands. If their right eyes should be put out, they would not be able to fight, and they would probably become slaves forever.

"Give us seven days to send messengers throughout Israel," they told the commander. "Then if no one comes forth to help us we will become your slaves."

The messengers were sent out, and when they came to Gibeah where Saul lived, they told the people. All who heard the news wept. Saul, who still followed his customary life-style, was out plowing his field when he heard the wailing of the people.

"What is wrong?" he asked.

"The Ammonites have attacked the people of Jabesh-gilead," the messengers said. "The people will be killed unless they consent to have their right eyes put out."

"This will not happen," declared Saul, his face becoming red with anger.

At once he took his pair of oxen and cut them to pieces. Then he gave the pieces to the messengers and sent them throughout all Israel. "Whoever does not come and follow Saul and Samuel," he stressed, "this will be done to his oxen."

Three hundred thousand men reported from Israel and thirty thousand came from Judah. When the messengers returned to Jabesh-gilead and told the people help was on the way, the town leaders sent word to the Ammonites.

"Tomorrow we will come out to you and you can do with us as you please."

Meanwhile Saul divided his men into three companies. They entered the Ammonite camp before dawn, killed many of the Ammonites, and scattered the survivors so that no two were together. Then all the people praised Saul.

"See, we told you a king would be good for us," they told Samuel. "See what he has done."

"God has brought the deliverance to Israel," corrected Saul.

"Come, let's go to Gilgal and renew the kingdom," Samuel said to the people.

They went to Gilgal where they offered peace offerings before God and rejoiced over their victory and their new king. Still, Samuel knew that a king for Israel was not God's perfect plan for them, and he let them know that the responsibility was neither his nor theirs.

"I have listened to you in all you've said and have anointed a king over you. See, here he is. He walks before you now and I am old and gray. I have walked before you from my childhood until this day. Who of you can accuse me of stealing, or oppressing anyone, or taking a bribe? Tell me and I will restore what is yours."

"You have not stolen from us or oppressed us or taken bribes," the people answered.

"God has heard you say that this day," Samuel declared.

"Yes, that is right," the people affirmed.

"I'm going to tell you how good God has been to you," Samuel continued. "When our forefather Jacob and his sons were in Egypt and the Egyptians oppressed them, they cried to God, and God sent Moses and Aaron to lead them out of Egypt to dwell here in this land. When the people forgot God, he allowed the Philistines and the Moabites to fight against them. The people at last cried to God and said, 'We have sinned because we have forgotten you, and have served other gods, but please deliver us now and we will serve only you.' God then sent you judges and prophets, yes, even me, and you were delivered from your enemies. But now when the Ammonites came against you, you said, 'Let our king deliver us,' when it was God who had delivered you before. Hear this, King Saul, and all you people: If you will fear God and serve him, listen to him and do not rebel against his commandments, it will go well for you. If you will not listen to God's voice, and rebel against him, his hand will be against you as it was against your fathers."

Then Samuel stood apart from the people.

"Stand still now and see a great thing God will do before your eyes," he shouted. "Is it not wheat harvest time? I will call to God and he will bring thunder and rain so you'll know that your wickedness in asking for a king is great before God."

Samuel called to God and he sent thunder and rain, and the people were greatly afraid of God and Samuel.

"We have sinned," they cried, shielding their heads. "Pray for us so we won't die. Now we see how great our sin of asking for a king is in God's eyes."

"Don't be afraid," Samuel said tenderly. "Just follow God. Don't put your faith in worthless things that can't deliver you. God won't forsake you. He has chosen you to be his people. And I won't forsake you either. I will continue to pray for you and to instruct you in the right way. Just remember how good God has been to you and serve him faithfully. But," he warned them, "if you do wickedly, you and your king will be swept away."

You Decide

1. When you are tempted to do wrong, do you try to make a compromise or do you call on God for help.
2. For what things in your life are you totally responsible?
3. For what part of your life are your parents still responsible?
4. In what ways was Samuel like a parent to Saul and the Israelites?

V

As the years went by, Samuel's words became very significant and Saul's behavior caused Samuel to grieve over him. Saul seemed to have everything going for him at the beginning, but he began to be slack in his dependence upon God, choosing instead to make his own decisions as king.

Such was the case in another battle, this time with the Philistines. Saul called together the men of Israel to meet him in Gilgal. Three thousand men came to Saul, but when the Philistines gathered for battle, they had thirty thousand chariots, six thousand horsemen, and more men than could be counted. The Israelites were frightened. Some hid in caves, holes, rocks, tombs, and pits and some went home. Others followed Saul to Gilgal, trembling all the way.

Samuel was still Saul's spiritual guide. He had told Saul to wait for seven days for him to come. "I will come and offer the sacrifice to God before we go into battle," he had said.

As the seven days progressed, Saul's impatience at having to wait for the old man turned to anxiety. The enemy was advancing and his troops were beginning to scatter. Still Samuel did not come.

"Come," Saul told the men. "I will offer the sacrifice myself. If Samuel comes before we go, he can bless us."

105

Saul took upon himself the function of a priest and prepared and sacrificed the burnt offering to God. Just as he finished, Samuel arrived. Saul went out to meet him, but Samuel's greeting was not what Saul expected.

"What have you done?" Samuel asked sternly.

"The Philistines were closing in on us. The men wanted to go to battle and I hadn't asked God's help yet, so I forced myself to offer a burnt offering."

"You have acted foolishly," Samuel said, obviously filled with disappointment. "You have not obeyed God's command. He would have established your kingdom forever, but now he will find another man, a man who will be obedient. He will make him king instead of you."

Rebuked, Saul retreated to his men. Counting them again, he found there were only six hundred. Furthermore, only Saul and his son Jonathan had swords. There was no way the Israelites could win this battle.

"Let's go up and spy out the Philistine garrison," Jonathan said to his armor-bearer. Without telling Saul, they climbed the rocks to spy on the enemy. Jonathan devised a plan. After they let the Philistines see them, if the enemy called to them to stay there, they would stay. If the enemy said to come on up, they would know God had delivered the Philistines into their hands.

Jonathan and his armor-bearer climbed up the rocks to where the enemy could see them. The Philistines began whispering together and pointing at them. "Come up to us," they called.

"Climb up after me," Jonathan whispered to his armor-bearer while he kept his eyes fastened on the enemy. "God has given them into Israel's hand."

Jonathan climbed up with his armor-bearer, and the Philistines began to fall before Jonathan. In all he and his armor-bearer killed about twenty men. Just then God caused an earthquake and the remaining Philistines panicked.

Saul, hearing the commotion, looked up and saw the Philistines scattering.

"Who is missing from among us?" he asked.

When they counted, they found Jonathan and his armor-bearer were missing. As the noise from the Philistines increased, Saul and all the people around him and those who had hidden, rallied and went into battle. God delivered Israel that day and the Philistines were driven back.

A curious thing happened later with the Israelite army. Saul had made all his men take an oath that they would not eat until evening and until they had defeated the enemy. As they came to a wooded area, they found a hive with honey dripping from it. The men, even though they were tired and faint, did not take any because they feared the oath. Jonathan had not been there when Saul had given these orders and he dipped into the honeycomb and ate some of it. Then the men told him that Saul had cursed anyone who did this.

"My father was wrong in doing that," said Jonathan. "See how much more alert I am after eating. If the men had been allowed to take some of the food from the enemy as they went along, we could have fought better and destroyed more Philistines."

When night came, the men were so hungry that they took animals from the enemy camp, slew them, and began to eat them raw simply because it was the fastest thing they could get.

"The men are sinning against God by eating with the blood," someone told Saul. Saul immediately sent word that they should bring their food to one central place and prepare it according to God's laws.

After they ate, Saul decided they should pursue the Philistines farther that night and he asked God's counsel. God didn't answer him, nor did he answer him the next day. Saul called all the chief men together.

"Let's find out who has sinned so against God that he will not answer us," he said. "Whoever has caused this will surely die."

They drew lots and the lot fell to Jonathan.

"Tell me what you have done," Saul said to his son.

"I tasted some honey," answered Jonathan, "and now I am condemned to die."

"Yes," said Saul. "You must die because of the curse."

All the people said, "Shall the one who led us in this victory over the Philistines die? God forbid! He shall not be hurt. It was he who brought this great deliverance today with God."

The people rescued Jonathan from Saul.

As Samuel watched Saul's progress as king he detected a disturbing pattern. Saul had started out well. Then he had made the sacrifice on his own before the battle. And now his bad judgment had led him to an unbending position on a fanatical oath. What would he do next? Would he turn back to trusting God, or would he further risk not only his crown but the lives of his people as he led them in the wrong direction. Still Samuel prayed for Saul and loved him and continued to admonish him to listen and to heed God's words.

You Decide

1. *Instead of waiting for Samuel to come and offer the sacrifice to God, what did Saul do?*

2. *What foolish promise did Saul want the men to make?*

3. *Why was Saul going to have Jonathan killed?*

4. *Do you think Saul was relying on God's direction or making his own decisions?*

5. *Pretend that you are Samuel and describe your feelings as you watch Saul and the Israelites choose a path away from God.*

VI

God knows when peoples' hearts are hardened beyond repentance. He knew this about the Amalekites. When the nation of Israel came out of Egypt and journeyed to Canaan, the Amalekites tried to hinder them on their way. Now in Samuel's time these people were not only hostile to Israel but proved themselves ripe for God's judgment. Samuel, in his role of prophet, told Saul that God was going to use him to punish the Amalekites.

"You are to completely destroy all the Amalekites including all their flocks and herds," Samuel told Saul.

Usually God had allowed the Israelites to take spoil from their enemies, but this time was different.

Saul assembled his men and waited in a valley. He saw that there were other people with the Amalekites. These were the Kenite people who had shown kindness to the Israelites when the Amalekites had not. Saul told the Kenites to leave so that they would not be destroyed along with the Amalekites. When they left, Saul went in and did destroy the people completely except that he took Agag, the Amalekite king, alive. He and his people also kept the best of the sheep, oxen, cattle, lambs, and all that was good.

"It would be a shame to destroy these," Saul decided, "but I have obeyed God in destroying all the people and most of the animals."

Then as Samuel waited at his home to hear news of the battle, God told him, "I regret making Saul king for he will not follow me or obey my commands."

This grieved Samuel deeply. He must have wondered how this could be if God had chosen Saul to be the king. He knew God doesn't make mistakes. Perhaps he even blamed himself for failing to instruct and warn Saul enough. Samuel had prayed for Saul constantly and he prayed for him now. He didn't want Saul to fail. He wanted him to turn back and follow God.

God, however, told Samuel, "I'm now going to use another way to lead my people. I will no longer work through Saul."

Samuel got up early the next morning to meet Saul, but he was told, "Saul came to Carmel to set up a monument to himself and has now gone to Gilgal."

Samuel too went to Gilgal to meet Saul.

"I have done what God commanded," Saul greeted him cheerfully.

"What then is this bleating of sheep and lowing of oxen that I hear?" demanded Samuel.

Saul stopped short, searching for the right words. He could see Samuel's disapproval.

"The people spared the best of the Amalekite sheep and oxen to sacrifice to God," he said with a touch of innocence in his voice, "but we have destroyed the rest."

"I will tell you what God said to me last night," Samuel said. "When you were small in your own eyes, God picked you out and made you king over Israel. Then he gave you a task to go and destroy the Amalekites."

Saul's eyes could not meet Samuel's steady gaze.

"Saul, Saul," Samuel said miserably, "why didn't you obey God instead of taking what he told you to destroy?"

"I have obeyed God," insisted Saul. "I destroyed all of the Amalekites and have brought back Agag, their king. But the people took the spoil, the best of the animals, to sacrifice to God in Gilgal."

"Does God want sacrifice rather than obedience?" Samuel said, once more trying to reach Saul. "No, Saul, God wants you to obey him, for rebellion against God is as bad as witchcraft. In his eyes, stubbornness is as bad as worshiping idols."

Saul had been proud of his success. Everyone was following him and acclaiming his victory. Now he wavered.

"Because you have rejected God's word," Samuel concluded, "he has rejected you from being king."

Hearing the finality in Samuel's voice, Saul was overcome by sorrow. "I have sinned," he confessed. "I have not obeyed God. I feared the people and I obeyed their voice." Kneeling before Samuel, he begged, "Please pardon me and go back with me so I can worship God."

"I will not go with you," Samuel sighed. "You have rejected God's word, and God has rejected you from being king over Israel."

Samuel turned to go. Saul, grabbing for him, seized his robe and tore it. Samuel stopped and looked longingly at Saul.

"God has torn the kingdom from your hands and has given it to someone better than you. God means what he says."

"I have sinned," Saul said desperately, "but honor me now before the elders and all the people. Come back with me so I can worship God."

"Come," said Samuel.

The two walked slowly back to the people who had gathered to worship. Samuel offered the sacrifice to God with a heavy heart. Saul was trying to believe everything was all right between him and God as he joined the worship.

Then Samuel said, "Bring me Agag, the king of the Amalekites."

Agag, relieved that his life had been spared, came readily to Samuel.

"Just as you have made many women childless by your sword," Samuel said to him, "so now I will make your mother childless."

There before all the people Samuel did what God had commanded Saul to do. He took a sword and killed Agag, king of the Amalekites.

After this Samuel went home to Ramah, and Saul went to his home in Gilgal. Samuel never again went to see Saul, but his grief for him was deep.

You Decide

1. *God's direction to Saul concerning the Amalekites clear?*

2. *Explain this sentence: "God wants obedience not sacrifice."*

3. *Do you think Saul was really repentant? Check your answer by reading about the rest of Saul's life in First Samuel.*

4. *How do you think Samuel measured his success or failure in life at this moment?*

VII

"How long are you going to grieve over Saul seeing that I have rejected him as king over Israel?" God said to Samuel. "Come, fill your horn with oil and I will send you to Bethlehem, to a man named Jesse. I have chosen one of his sons to be king of my people."

Samuel was afraid. "How can I do this?" he objected. "If Saul finds out, he will kill me."

"Take a heifer and go to Bethlehem to offer a sacrifice," God said. "Ask Jesse and his sons to join you, and I will show you what to do. I will reveal to you which one to anoint as my king."

Samuel took the heifer and journeyed to Bethlehem. There he found Jesse and asked him to bring his sons to the sacrifice. When they were all assembled, Samuel asked to meet each of Jesse's sons. Jesse first introduced Eliab, his eldest son. When Samuel saw him he thought that Eliab was surely the one God had chosen. But God would teach Samuel a lesson.

"Samuel, don't look at his outward appearance," God said, "how handsome he is, how tall and straight. That is the way man judges. God looks at the man's heart, and I have not chosen this man."

Next Jesse introduced Abinadab.

"God has not chosen him either," said Samuel.

Then Jesse introduced Shammah, but Samuel again said, "God has not chosen him."

Jesse brought seven of his sons to Samuel. Samuel was puzzled.

"God has not chosen any of these," he said. "Are these all of your sons?"

"There is one more," Jesse answered, "the youngest. He is out tending the sheep."

"Bring him to me," Samuel urged. "We will not sit down to eat until he comes."

Jesse sent for David, his youngest son, and brought him to Samuel.

"This is the one," said God. "Anoint him."

Samuel took the horn of oil and anointed David in the midst of his brothers and from that time forward the Spirit of God was on David. David, however, did not assume leadership of his nation at that time. Saul was still in command. But the Bible says that from that time on, the Spirit of God left Saul and he began to have times of anxiety and even rage. He increasingly became jealous of David who seemed so favored by God and later by the people. David meanwhile let God train him in courage as he guarded the sheep, in leadership as he fought in Saul's army, and in integrity toward Saul as he waited for God's timing. David became Israel's greatest king, and God said he "followed me with all his heart" (I Kings 14:8 NIV).

Samuel lived a life of obedience and service to God, and God used him as a judge and later as a prophet for the people. God authorized him to anoint Israel's first king and to be a guide to him. God commanded that he anoint Israel's greatest king, David. Little did Hannah realize when she asked for a son and later when she dedicated him to God and left him at the temple, what wonderful privileges God had in store for Samuel.

Of Samuel's death, the Bible says only that he died and all Israel assembled and mourned for him. Samuel was buried in Ramah, his hometown.

You Decide

1. *How does God choose someone to do his work?*
2. *For what did God ask Samuel to be responsible?*
3. *For what were the people responsible?*

4.

CHOSEN TO REIGN, CHOSEN TO SERVE

I

For you created my inmost being;
  you knit me together in my mother's womb.
I praise you because I am fearfully and
    wonderfully made;
  your works are wonderful,
  I know that full well.
My frame was not hidden from you
  when I was made in the secret place.
When I was woven together in the depths of the
    earth,
  your eyes saw my unformed body.
All the days ordained for me
  were written in your book
  before one of them came to be.

(Psalm 139:13-16 NIV)

"For we are God's workmanship, created in Christ Jesus to do good works, which God prepared in advance for us to do" (Ephesians 2:10 NIV).

God knew you before you were born. God knew the circumstances of your birth. God knew the family in which you would be reared, and God knows the path of life that will make you happiest.

Before you were born God began to set the stage for your entrance into life. He moved people and circumstances so that when it came time for you to be on earth's stage, all was in readiness.

So it was with Esther's life. See if you can follow all the circumstances that resulted in her saving her people.

In the year 586 B.C. the Jews in Judah were conquered and put in chains by King Nebuchadnezzar and taken captive to Babylon. For seventy years they lived as captives in that land. In 539 B.C. the Medes and Persians conquered the Babylonians. As a result, the Jews were further scattered into all the provinces of Persia. During the reign of Cyrus, king of Persia, the Jews were given permission to return to their land and rebuild the temple in Jerusalem. This decree was sent to all the places where the Jews had been scattered, and approximately 50,000 returned to Jerusalem. The bulk of the nation chose to remain where they were. By now they had made friends with their captors and were leading comfortable lives. They had settled down and had established trades. Some had probably intermarried with the Persians (which was forbidden by God) and children had been born to them in captivity. Undoubtedly, Esther was born during this period. In any event, the first time we meet her is in Shushan, Persia's capital, where she lived with her older cousin, Mordecai.

King Ahasuerus (or Xerxes) was now king of the Persian Empire. His empire stretched from India to Ethiopia and had 127 provinces. Indeed his kingdom was the largest the world had ever seen.

"I will have a great feast for all my princes, army officers, and governors," declared the king. "I will show them all the riches I have gathered."

The plans were made and the announcements sent out. The feast lasted for six months. King Ahasuerus was actually planning to enlarge his kingdom by invading Greece. Perhaps this was his way of convincing all his important people that this could easily be afforded.

Near the end of this feast he had a seven-day feast for all the people in his capital city of Shushan. They were all invited to his palace which was very elaborately decorated with fine linen cloths and with couches of gold and silver set on floors of marble and precious stones. The people were served as much wine as they wanted in golden goblets.

The queen, Vashti, also gave a banquet for all the royal ladies of the palace.

On the seventh day of the feast, when the king had finally had too much partying and too much wine, he did a foolish thing. He decided to have his servants get the queen so he could show her off to his guests for she was very beautiful. Now this was not a courteous thing to do nor was it in any way considered good manners in that day. Most of the men were drunk. Besides that, what queen would want to be shown off to a bunch of men as part of the king's "riches"? Vashti, the queen, refused to go.

Embarrassed and angry, the king demanded, "What should we do to Queen Vashti since she has refused to do what the king has asked of her? What is the law?"

"This refusal of the queen to come when the king calls could cause problems around the whole kingdom," one of his counselors said in alarm. "When the other women hear of this they will think they don't have to obey their husbands."

"I propose," another said, "that the king make a royal decree to divorce Vashti and choose another wife. Furthermore, the decree that the king makes should be written into the law of the Medes and Persians."

Any law written in the law of the Medes and Persians could not be changed. It could not be voted out. It was law forever and ever. The king made his decree and it was proclaimed throughout his kingdom.

All wives are to give honor to their husbands. Every man shall rule his own house and furthermore he shall speak his own language in his house. If he has married foreign wives, they are to learn his language.

Vashti was divorced and banished from the palace. Later on when the king was no longer angry, he remembered Vashti. He may even have longed for her to return.

"There must be beautiful young ladies around the kingdom from whom the king could choose a new queen," suggested one of his counselors.

The counselor's suggestion pleased the king and arrangements were made to bring the most beautiful young women in the kingdom to the palace for the king to see.

You Decide

1. *How did some of the Jews happen to live in Persia?*
2. *Who was the king of Persia?*
3. *How did the king convince his officials that he was wealthy?*
4. *Describe what happened to Queen Vashti.*
5. *How did the king plan to get a new queen?*

II

During this time Mordecai, a Jewish refugee, lived in the capital city of Shushan. Mordecai and his family had been carried away captive when Nebuchadnezzar conquered Jerusalem. When his uncle and aunt were killed, Mordecai took their child, Esther, to rear as his own daughter. Esther was a beautiful young lady.

In Shushan Mordecai had gained political favor with his captors and was given a position as an attendant in the king's court. When he saw the beautiful young maidens being brought into the palace to vie for the king's favor, he considered his adopted daughter, Esther.

She is more beautiful than all the others, he thought. Besides, Esther is not only lovely, but sensible and wise. Esther would be a marvelous queen. She could easily be chosen by the king.

Esther also was taken to the king's house. There she was put under the charge of Hegai, keeper of the women.

Mordecai was really taking a terrible chance with Esther's life when he encouraged this. For one thing, Jews were forbidden by God to marry non-Jews. For another thing, if Esther were not chosen to be queen, she would live the rest of her life in the king's harem.

Esther, however, pleased Hegai, her keeper. He, too, noted that she was beautiful, but he also detected a queenly quality in her. He gave her not only the provisions decreed by the king but also seven maids. He separated her from the other young ladies and put her in the best apartment in the harem. There Esther lived for one year undergoing beauty treatments.

Finally, the time came for the maidens to be presented to the king. Each one was presented by herself but she could take anything she desired with her to entice the king. Esther was naturally beautiful and when it was her turn to be presented to the king, she took only what Hegai suggested. As Esther walked through the halls, all who saw her admired her great beauty and manner. The king, also, was completely charmed by Esther and he preferred her over any of the other maidens. He chose Esther for his queen and placed the crown on her head and gave a great feast in her honor.

During this time Esther had not revealed her nationality because Mordecai had told her not to. No one in the palace except Mordecai knew that she was a Jew.

One day as Mordecai sat at the king's gate he overheard a conversation between two of the king's servants. They were angry with the king and were plotting to kill him. Mordecai at once sent a message to Esther telling her of the scheme and Esther in turn told the king. She also told him that it was Mordecai who had overheard this. The king immediately ordered an investigation of the matter. When the allegation proved to be true, Mordecai was praised and the two servants were hanged. The whole incident was recorded in the king's journal.

There was another man in the kingdom who had distinguished himself before King Ahasuerus. His name was Haman. The king had promoted Haman above all the princes of the kingdom and had commanded that everyone was to bow down and do reverence to him when he passed by. All the king's servants who were at the king's gate bowed down to Haman except Mordecai. He did not bow down. Mordecai was a Jew, and although he may not have followed all of God's teachings to the Jews, he at least obeyed God's command, "You shall not have any gods before me. You shall not bow yourself down to them or serve them." No Jew would bow before another human.

Haman apparently did not notice Mordecai's disobedience but the other servants at the gate did.

"Why don't you bow down to Haman when it is the king's command to do so?" they asked Mordecai.

"I am a Jew," Mordecai told them. "I bow down only before the almighty God."

Every day his fellow servants spoke to him about this. Finally, the other servants told Haman about Mordecai. They may not have done this spitefully but merely to see if Haman would grant special privileges to Jews just because they were Jews. When Haman heard this, he made a point of watching Mordecai. Sure enough, when everyone else bowed down to him, Mordecai was still standing. Haman's eyes narrowed and his jaw tightened as he clenched his fists in anger.

"How could he have the audacity to refuse to bow to me? Try to embarrass me, will he? I will crush him like a man crushes an ant into the ground with his boot. I am Haman. I will not be ridiculed by a little Jew."

The next day Mordecai remained standing again as everyone else bowed to Haman. Haman could see the sideways glances of some of the other people.

"I will not be laughed at," Haman silently screamed in rage. "Not only will I ruin him, I will see that because of him, all other Jews are killed. I will not tolerate such insolence."

Haman immediately began to speculate on how he could accomplish such a thing. First, he needed the right timing. He decided to cast lots, or throw dice, to see when the right moment would be. This was rather like people in our day consulting palm readers or their astrological signs to determine when they should do something. He did this for a whole year and finally decided the deed should be done on the last month of the year. Second, he needed the king's approval for his plan which by now was firmly fixed in his mind. He went to the king.

"King Ahasuerus," he said, "there is a group of people dispersed throughout your land which has laws very different from all the other people of your kingdom. They do not even follow the laws you have made. Since they are really of no profit to you, you shouldn't even tolerate them. They do, however, have considerable possessions. Now I have a plan that will benefit both you and your kingdom. Let these people be destroyed and their possessions turned into the king's treasuries." Then he volunteered, "I will personally supervise this."

The king took off his signet ring that he used to seal his orders and gave it to Haman. "These people and their fate are in your hands," he said.

Notice that the king did not even inquire as to who these people were or how many people Haman was talking about. He was totally indifferent to them. He, like many kings in those days, was completely egotistical and had little regard for human life except as it benefited him.

The king's secretaries were called in on the thirteenth day of the first month of the year, and they wrote what Haman commanded. The notices were sent to all of the king's chief rulers, governors, and princes over the people of the provinces. Each was in the language of that province. The notices were sealed with the king's signet ring, and they were delivered by special messengers. This is what they said:

All Jews, both young and old, men and women and children, are to be destroyed in one day, the thirteenth day of the last month of the year, and their possessions are to be seized and delivered into the king's treasuries.

"How could this be?" wailed the Jewish people as they read the posted notice. "What have we done? Who has caused the king to react to us in this way? How can we and our little ones escape?"

The people mourned and fasted. Many put on rough goat's hair called sackcloth and covered their heads with ashes to show their grief. Mordecai also, when he learned all that had taken place, took off his fine clothes and dressed in sackcoth. He put ashes on his head and went through the city crying and mourning in a loud voice. He even stood before the king's gate dressed like that.

"Mordecai is standing at the king's gate dressed in sackcloth," Esther's servants told her.

Alarmed, Esther hurriedly gathered some clothes together and sent them out to Mordecai. "Tell him," she told the servant, "to let you take away the sackcloth."

Mordecai, however, would not take the clothes or even speak to the servant. Esther called Hathach, the servant she trusted most. "Go to Mordecai. Find out why he is grieving," she said.

When Hathach went out, Mordecai told him all that had happened, including the exact amount of silver Haman had promised to pay into the king's treasury to destroy the Jews. He also gave him a copy of the decree that had been circulated in Shushan.

"Go, explain this to Esther," lamented Mordecai. "Tell her to go to the king and plead with him for the lives of her people."

Frightened and dismayed at the report from Hathach, Esther sent this message back to Mordecai: "Everyone knows that no one is to approach the king unless he holds out his golden scepter to receive the person. If the king refuses to receive me I will be killed. Besides this, the king has not sent for me for thirty days. I don't know how he feels about me. I am afraid to go."

When Hathach told Mordecai Esther's answer, Mordecai returned this threefold message: "Do you think you can escape this same sentence of death just because you arc queen? If you don't help, deliverance for the Jews will come by someone else. Besides, who knows but that you came to the throne for just this purpose."

Esther dismissed Hathach and sat for a long time pondering this message. Finally, summoning her trusted servant once again, she replied to Mordecai. "Call all the Jews in Shushan together and fast for me for three days and nights. My maidens and I will do the same thing. Then I will go to the king. If I perish, I perish."

You Decide

1. *Do you think Mordecai was a good parent to Esther? Why?/Why not?*

2. *Why did King Ahasuerus choose Esther for his queen?*

3. *How was Mordecai repeatedly tempted day after day?*

4. *Who did Haman plot to kill?*

5. *Why do people consult palm readers, psychics, or astrological signs? What does God think of this? (See Leviticus 19:31 and Deuteronomy 18:9-12.)*

6. *Why was Esther afraid to tell the king of Haman's plan?*

7. *What purpose did Mordecai see in the fact that Esther, a Jew, was the queen?*

III

After three days Esther put on her royal robes and stood in the inner court of the palace. The king was sitting on his throne facing the entrance. He saw Esther when she came in. She was indeed beautiful and he loved her very much. My beautiful queen, he thought. How I've missed her these last few busy weeks.

"What is it you want, Queen Esther?" he lovingly asked, holding out his golden scepter to her. "You know that you have only to ask and I will give you up to half of my kingdom."

Esther approached, touched the tip of the scepter, and bowed. "If you will," she said, "I would like for you and Haman to come today to the banquet I have prepared for you."

"Of course we will come, my queen," the king replied. Summoning his servant, he told him to inform Haman at once of the queen's invitation.

The king and Haman came to Esther's dinner that day. During the serving of the wine the king again asked, "What is your request, Queen Esther? Ask and it will be granted to you even up to half of my kingdom."

"If it pleases the king to do so," Esther answered, "please come again tomorrow to the dinner I will prepare, both you and Haman. Tomorrow I will tell you my request."

Haman went away that day very proud and happy, but when he passed by Mordecai at the gate, Mordecai again stood while everyone else bowed. Haman's anger boiled up within him. He went home and called for his friends and his wife and told them of his good fortune at being the only one other than the king to be invited to the queen's banquet. "But," he added through clenched teeth, "none of this is worth anything as long as that Jew, Mordecai, refuses to bow down to me."

"The solution as I see it," sneered his wife, "is very simple. Why don't you erect a gallows? Go to the king tonight and tell him that Mordecai refuses to pay you respect. You could hang Mordecai in the morning and go to your dinner in peace."

Haman thought this was a good idea and, with his wife's encouragement, proceeded to have the gallows constructed.

That night King Ahasuerus could not sleep. He commanded that the book of the chronicles containing the recordings of the memorable deeds done in the kingdom be brought in and read to him. As the king's attendant was reading, he came across the account where Mordecai had reported to Esther the assassination plot on the king's life. The king sat up suddenly.

"What has been done to honor this man?" he asked.

"Nothing has been done," the attendant replied.

Just about that time, Haman entered the king's court. The king, still contemplating what to do for Mordecai, asked his servants if there was anyone in the court.

"Haman has come into the court," they answered.

"Good," said the king. "Let Haman come in."

As soon as he had entered, the king asked him, "What, in your opinion, should be done for someone whom the king wishes to honor?"

Haman thought the king must be talking about him. Smiling slightly, he straightened his shoulders and thrust out his chest. "Let him be dressed in royal robes worn by the king," he said. "Let a crown be put on his head. Let him be led on the king's horse through town by someone who cries aloud, 'This man is being honored by the king.'"

"Let it be so," King Ahasuerus replied. Then he added, "Do all just as you have said to Mordecai, the Jew."

Haman, shocked beyond belief, appalled and humiliated, was forced to lead the king's horse through the streets of Shushan. On the horse rode Mordecai, dressed in royal robes. Returning Mordecai to the palace, Haman covered his head in shame and rushed home. Mourning and whining pitifully, he told his wife and friends what had happened.

"Beware, Haman," they said. "If the king is honoring Mordecai who is a Jew, you'll not be able to get rid of him. In fact, he may get rid of you."

While they were still talking, the king's servants came to take Haman to the second banquet Esther had prepared for him and the king.

Esther looked especially beautiful that evening and the dinner was even more elaborate than the first one had been. Haman ate and drank greedily, but the king had eyes only for his lovely wife, Esther. "What is your request?" he asked. "Ask and it will be granted to you."

The time had come for Esther to make her request.

"I am pleading for my own life to be spared and those of my people," she began softly. "We have been sold and will be completely destroyed." Esther continued to tell the king all that had been decreed against the Jews. "If we were only to be made slaves I would not ask, but this order will surely damage the kingdom and the king's reputation."

"Who is he who has presumed in his heart to do this thing?" demanded the king.

"It is an enemy of the king," responded Esther. Then turning to point him out, she declared forcefully, "It is that wicked Haman!"

The king rose in anger. Staring first at Haman and then at Esther, he turned and quickly left the room to think. He was putting two and two together. So this was Haman's deceitful way of putting money into the king's treasury. His beautiful queen, a Jew, was to be destroyed in the process.

Meanwhile, gripped with panic, Haman could hardly breathe. His heart raced wildly and beads of perspiration dotted his forehead. How could he have known the queen was Jewish? To be humiliated by Mordecai was intolerable, but Esther obviously had power. What would she do to him? His eyes darted to the door where a slave stood at attention with a spear in his hand. Perhaps the queen will be merciful, he thought. Rushing to her couch he reached toward her imploringly. Esther shrank back from his grasp just as the king came back in. At the sight of Haman clutching his wife, the king called, "Seize him!"

The servants immediately rushed in, covered Haman's face with a hood, and took him out.

Then one of the attendants told the king, "There is a gallows seventy-five feet high that Haman just made."

"Hang him on it," ordered the king.

Without delay Haman was taken out and hanged on the gallows, the one he had prepared for Mordecai. With that the king's anger was pacified.

You Decide

1. Why do you think Esther didn't tell the king her request right away?

2. What did she gain by having two banquets for Haman and the king before making her request?

3. Mordecai's refusal to bow to Haman day after day was like a small constantly irritating thorn. What small, daily irritation upsets your life?

4. *What basic characteristic in Haman's life allowed this little thorn to become an all-consuming drive for revenge?*

5. *Was Haman's wife's counsel wise or unwise?*

6. *Are those who are close to you wise counselors or unwise?*

7. *Thus far in the story, do you think King Ahasuerus was a good king or a bad king? Why?*

8. *Would you like him for a father? Why?/ Why not? A teacher? Why?/Why not? A ruler? Why?/Why not?*

IV

On that day King Ahasuerus gave the house of Haman, the Jews' enemy, to Esther. Since Esther had revealed her nationality to King Ahasuerus, she now presented Mordecai to him as her cousin and guardian.

"Mordecai is the only family I have," she said. She told the king how Mordecai had reared her since her parents had died. Having already honored Mordecai for revealing the plot against his life, the king further honored him by giving him the signet ring that he had previously given to Haman. And Esther set Mordecai over the house of Haman.

Esther again came to the king in behalf of her people so the king might avert the plot of Haman to destroy the Jews. For even though Haman was dead, the Jews were still under the sentence of death. "How can I bear to see my people killed?" she pleaded.

The king said to Mordecai, "Write what you want concerning the Jews and seal it with my signet and send it out to all the provinces of my kingdom."

The king's scribes were called again and they wrote as Mordecai commanded them. The messages were delivered by riders to all the rulers, governors, and princes in the provinces from India to Ethiopia. This is what the message said:

On the thirteenth day of the twelfth month all Jews should gather together to defend themselves. By the king's command, Jews may destroy all who might attack them, their wives, and their little ones and should take the goods of the enemy as spoil.

The full power of the throne was behind this new decree. The king was on the side of the Jews. The original decree had not been altered in any way. It could not be, but now another decree was sent out under the full power of the king. The new decree provided a way of escape for the Jews. If they received the message in time and believed it, they could save their lives.

Rejoicing and shouting, the Jews did receive the messages and proclaimed a holiday and feast. By the time the thirteenth day of the twelfth month actually arrived, the Jews were gathered together in their cities throughout all the provinces of the kingdom to fight against anyone who sought to hurt them. There was no one who could defeat them. The people had become afraid of their strength. Furthermore, all the princes, governors, and chief rulers who were employed in the king's business helped the Jews because they were afraid of Mordecai, who had become very powerful in the king's palace.

In the capital city of Shushan, the Jews killed five hundred men who attacked them. They also killed the ten sons of Haman, the enemy of the Jews.

When King Ahasuerus heard all the news from Shushan, he again called for Esther, his queen. "Now," he said, "do you have a further request? Tell me and it will be done."

Esther, sensing that there might be reprisals from the enemy the next day, said, "Let the Jews again defend themselves tomorrow and let the bodies of Haman's ten sons hang on the gallows as a witness to the people."

On the fourteenth day of the twelfth month the Jews of Shushan again defended themselves against their enemies but did not take any spoil. The bodies of Haman's sons were hanged on the gallows for all to see. The following day there was peace and the people rested and rejoiced.

After that Queen Esther and Mordecai sent a letter to all the Jews in the provinces that they should remember this event yearly. To this day, the Jewish people celebrate what they call the Feast of Purim named after Pur which means "lot" because Haman had cast lots to determine the day he would destroy the Jews. Esther is remembered as the queen who saved her people.

You Decide

1. *Do you understand how the crisis caused by Haman was corrected?*
   a. *Was the original decree by Haman changed? Why?/Why not?*
   b. *What way of escape was provided for the Jews?*
   c. *What did the Jews actually have to do?*
2. *God has declared that all humankind must die because all are sinners. Do you know his second decree that provides a way of escape?*
3. *How many coincidences in Esther's life can you recall that resulted in Esther's saving her people from destruction?*

ADOPTED AS GOD'S CHILD

For I know the plans I have for you," declares the Lord, "plans to prosper you and not to harm you, plans to give you hope and a future" (Jeremiah 29:11 NIV).

In this world of uncertainty and constant change, where can a person find calmness and light in a violent storm, an anchor that holds firmly, a solid foundation on which to stand? Is there anyone who knows for sure which way you should go when the road forks or which path will bring you the most contentment? Does anyone care how you really feel deep down inside when you're all alone?

All of us long to be thoroughly known by someone and at the same time thoroughly loved in spite of our faults. Where can we go? Who can we trust? Is there an ultimate companion in whom we can place so much loyalty and confidence?

It would have been easy for Joseph to despair when his own family members sold him into a land from which he could probably never return or see his father again. It would have been easy for Joseph to say God did not see or else did not care that his moral integrity was rewarded with two years of imprisonment. It would have been easy for Joseph to take his own revenge on his brothers when at last they were together, for he was next in power to Pharaoh. But Joseph saw that God had orchestrated all his days, both the good and the bad, to help preserve his family, God's people. God had picked Joseph from his eleven brothers for just that special purpose, and Joseph could piece these events together as he looked back on his life.

God's purpose for Esther and Moses was to lead God's people away from certain destruction. Condemned to die by an unchangeable decree written by her king, Esther pleaded for her life and the lives of her people. In mercy the king wrote another decree. This decree did not erase the sentence of death, but overruled it, allowing the Jews to live.

Likewise during Moses' lifetime God provided a way for his people to escape slavery. First, in response to God's command, they marked their doorposts with the blood of a lamb. Then they followed Moses through the parted waters of the Red Sea to freedom.

Even though God made provision to rescue his people, the choice to act on such provision was left to Esther and to Moses. Physical death was imminent when Esther chose to act. A life of enslavement engulfed the Israelites when Moses chose to act. In each case, God was faithful, moving people and circumstances, to provide a fulfilled life for his chosen people.

Hannah, in her sorrow, asked for life from God. God gave her Samuel. Hannah later placed that life back in God's hands, and Samuel became one of God's greatest prophets.

Your life is also a gift *from* God. What you choose to do with your life is your gift *to* God. Finding the unique purpose for which he created you and by which you will find your deepest joy, involves a major decision on your part and that is what this chapter is all about.

God is an expert at calming storms, bringing light into the darkness, and holding firmly onto uncertain hands. He alone provides a firm, non-slippery foundation on which to stand. God says, "Follow me. I know all the roads. I will lead you in truth and in love. I have felt all that you have felt. In fact my understanding of you is complete and perfect because I made you. I love you."

This is the same God that Joseph, Moses, Samuel, and Esther worshiped. He is perfect in knowledge and love, and he is the one who wants to adopt you as his own child.

God invites each of us to come and be part of his family, a brother or sister to Joseph, Moses, Samuel, Esther, and others you may know right now. He calls you. Are you listening? Have you felt his Holy Spirit prompt you to respond?

When I was a child, I learned that God loved me so much that he sent his only Son, Jesus, to die on a cross for my sins. The only way I could be clean and pure before a holy God was to accept Jesus' sacrifice as being personally for me. He died in my place. I believed that, and it was like putting the blood of a lamb on my doorpost so that the angel of death would pass over me. It was like receiving a new decree to supersede the old decree under which I was condemned.

As an adopted child of God, I have all the rights and privileges of a family member. I am a joint heir with Jesus Christ, God's only Son, inheriting all his spiritual riches, including peace and joy. Through prayer I have direct access to God at any time, and he encourages my questions as well as my worship. His Holy Spirit is constantly with me carefully guiding me within the boundaries he has set. I am like a precious jewel to him. God has drawn a hedge of protection round me. He does not deal with me according to what I deserve; instead, in love and mercy God trains and disciplines me. One day, when my physical body dies, I will go to the place he has prepared especially for me. There I will live throughout eternity encircled in his love.

How should you respond to God's invitation? Right now you can choose by faith to open your life to him. If you do that, God promises to come into your life and adopt you as his own child forever. He will assure you that he loves you and that you are now his own child by giving you his Holy Spirit, sometimes called the "Spirit of Adoption." Through God's Word, the Bible, he will feed your mind spiritual food daily as he miraculously fed the Israelites in the desert. God will defend you from the enemy because you are his own dear child. He will satisfy your thirst for truth, and as you follow his leading, God will give you the desires of your heart.

Hallelujah, I am adopted! There's plenty of room in God's family for you.

"In love he predestined us to be adopted as his sons through Jesus Christ" (Ephesians 1:5 NIV).